18541

D1121896

Library
Oakland S.U.M.

VICTORIOUS CHRISTIAN SERVICE

VICTORIOUS CHRISTIAN SERVICE

Studies in the Book of Nehemiah

by ALAN REDPATH

FLEMING H. REVELL COMPANY

2213

COPYRIGHT © MCMLVIII, BY FLEMING H. REVELL COMPANY

All Rights Reserved

Printed in the United States of America

Library of Congress Catalog Card Number: 58-11020

Westwood, New Jersey

1.4

*Dedicated to my beloved wife
whose faithfulness and consistency
have been a constant source of inspiration
in the service of the Lord*

Foreword

THERE IS NO type of service any of us can undertake which is beset with so much potential as is the service of the Master. On the one hand, there is so much that is rewarding, and on the other hand, so much that is disappointing. Many are the obstacles to be overcome and many the pitfalls to be avoided. On how many occasions we have taken up a task in the name of the Lord only to withdraw, beaten, discouraged, and baffled, and yet, somehow, baffled to fight better. For every discouragement has been allowed to come to us in order that through it we may be cast in utter helplessness at the Saviour's feet. Then we return to the battle again, no longer trusting in the false and insufficient human resources which so foolishly we had taken into the battle, but now trusting in the limitless resources of our risen Lord.

Never was there a time when there was a greater need for men of passion, men of principle, men of Holy Spirit vision, in the service of the Lord. It is impossible for any of us to become any of these things unless first we have stood in the midst of the work which the Master has given to us and have seen the futility of everything that can ever come from our own imagined strength or weakness. These are lessons which most of us learn the hard way, and we learn them in a school from which we never graduate until we enter the very presence of the Master Himself.

It is my earnest prayer that this little book may be used in some way to help others to avoid some of the pitfalls and to triumph in some of the challenging situations which confront them. It contains much that the Lord has been teaching me in the crucible of my own ministry. But as I think of the title of the book itself, I am humbled indeed, and would be careful to say, in the words of the Apostle Paul, "Not as though I had already attained, either were already perfect: but I follow after, if that I may apprehend that for which also I am apprehended of Christ Jesus."

It is my firm conviction, based not only upon what I believe to be the teaching of Scripture but upon my own experience—limited though it has been—that, in choosing us in Christ before the foundation of the world, our Heavenly Father also had in His eternal plan the sphere of service with which He intended to entrust us. In doing so, surely He had in mind that through our reaction in all the testings of Christian work and through our faithfulness or lack of it in the opportunities that He is pleased to give us, we are fashioned into the likeness of His dear Son. If the messages of this book reach the hands and the hearts of some of God's servants who are going through the fire and bring them encouragement, renewed hope, and vision, leading them into the reality of victory in the Lord Jesus, then I believe its publication will have been abundantly worth while.

Once again I would express to Miss Arline Harris my most grateful thanks for her proficient and thorough preparation of the manuscript.

ALAN REDPATH
Moody Memorial Church

Chicago, Illinois

Contents

	FOREWORD	7
1.	RECOGNIZING THE NEED	13
2.	PREPARATION AND EQUIPMENT	27
3.	FACING THE CHALLENGE	41
4.	THE STARTING POINT FOR ALL	55
5.	OVERCOMING THE FOE	67
6.	REMOVING RUBBISH	81
7.	BUILDING AND BATTLING	93
8.	STEERING CLEAR OF TROUBLE	107
9.	TOTAL CHRISTIAN WARFARE	121
10.	STRENGTH FOR THE BATTLE	135
11.	SOME PRINCIPLES OF REVIVAL	149
12.	STRATEGY AND SURRENDER	165
13.	A GRAND FINALE	179

VICTORIOUS CHRISTIAN SERVICE

I. Recognizing the Need

The words of Nehemiah the son of Hachaliah. And it came to pass in the month Chisleu, in the twentieth year, as I was in Shushan the palace,

That Hanani, one of my brethren, came, he and certain men of Judah; and I asked them concerning the Jews that had escaped, which were left of the captivity, and concerning Jerusalem.

And they said unto me, The remnant that are left of the captivity there in the province are in great affliction and reproach: the wall of Jerusalem also is broken down, and the gates thereof are burned with fire.

And it came to pass, when I heard these words, that I sat down and wept, and mourned certain days, and fasted, and prayed before the God of heaven,

And said, I beseech thee, O Lord God of heaven, the great and terrible God, that keepeth covenant and mercy for them that love him and observe his commandments:

Let thine ear now be attentive, and thine eyes open, that thou mayest hear the prayer of thy servant, which I pray before thee now, day and night, for the children of Israel thy servants, and confess the sins of the children of Israel, which we have sinned against thee: both I and my father's house have sinned.

We have dealt very corruptly against thee, and have not kept the commandments, nor the statutes, or the judgments, which thou commandedst thy servant Moses.

Remember, I beseech thee, the word that thou com-

mandedst thy servant Moses, saying, If ye transgress, I will scatter you abroad among the nations:

But if ye turn unto me, and keep my commandments, and do them; though there were of you cast out unto the uttermost part of the heaven, yet will I gather them from thence, and will bring them unto the place that I have chosen to set my name there.

Now these are thy servants and thy people, whom thou hast redeemed by thy great power, and by thy strong hand.

O Lord, I beseech thee, let now thine ear be attentive to the prayer of thy servant, and to the prayer of thy servants, who desire to fear thy name: and prosper, I pray thee, thy servant this day, and grant him mercy in the sight of this man. For I was the king's cupbearer.

—Nehemiah 1:1-11

THE BOOK OF NEHEMIAH is perhaps the classic of the whole Bible on the subject of personal service for God.

To enter a business career, to study for any profession, to go to the uttermost part of the earth to preach the gospel, to enter the ministry, to begin to teach a Sunday school class—to do *any* service for God without regard for what may be the will of God, without understanding the real principles of Christian service, is not only foolish but sinful. Why? Because to do that asserts the right to choose your own task, your own sphere of service, your own life, and ignores the claims of the Saviour, which should take first place.

As we turn to this book, I pray that the Holy Spirit will burn into all our hearts that the Lord Jesus Christ has the supreme claim upon the life of each one of us. May you make your prayer as you read these messages, "Lord, what wilt Thou have me to do, and how wilt Thou have me to do it?"

Only insofar as every part of your life is adjusted to God in every detail can God achieve His purpose through you, and only as He achieves His purpose through you will your life be successful in the truest sense of the word. We ought to pray, therefore, as we turn to this book, that many of us will be led into a clear knowledge of the will

15

of God and that all of us will be brought to understand more fully the principles of all Christian work.

In order that we may catch the full significance of this Book of Nehemiah, we need to be clear as to the particular circumstances in which it was written and the period of history to which it refers. Of the seventeen historical books in the Bible, the most recent in date are Ezra, Esther and Nehemiah. Ezra and Nehemiah are both divided into two parts. The first six chapters of Ezra have to do with the rebuilding of the temple; the last four chapters have to do with the restoration of worship. Sixty years elapsed between Ezra's first six chapters and the last four chapters. In those sixty years occurred the events recorded in the Book of Esther, when the preservation of the whole Jewish race was at stake. The first six chapters of the Book of Nehemiah have to do with the reconstruction of the walls of Jerusalem and the last seven chapters have to do with the re-instruction of the people of God.

The historical events which were unfolding during this time were of great interest and of deep spiritual significance. The Jewish people had been taken into captivity for seventy years in Babylon, but in the year 530 B.C. the power of the Babylonian Empire was broken by the power of Persia, and upon assuming supremacy, the king of Persia encouraged the Jewish remnant to return to their own country and to the city of Jerusalem.

Immediately some fifty thousand of them did return, and they set about the immense task of rebuilding the temple, which was so vital to the life of the Jewish people in their worship of God. Discouraged by opposition from the people who had settled in that particular country during the years of their captivity, and also by the immensity of the task, the Jews soon abandoned the work with only the foundation of the temple rebuilt.

About sixteen years later, when all the people had settled down to dwell in their own homes, God raised up two men, Haggai and Zechariah, who challenged the people concerning their way of life and pointed out their neglect of the things of God. The people were inspired by the ministry of these two men and the work of the reconstruction of the temple was again commenced. This time it was completed, some twenty years after the first group had returned from captivity.

Sixty more years passed by, and then a further section of the Jewish people returned to Jerusalem under the leadership of Ezra himself in the year 458 B.C. This man, a priest who traced his ancestry back to Aaron, set about re-establishing the moral and spiritual life of the people who for so long had lived in that land in such a deplorable state. Ezra entered upon that task with a great deal of discouragement from other people; much remained to be done. They were challenged on every hand by the people who lived in the country. The Persian king who had sent them back had no power to send them reinforcements, with the result that for more than ninety years after the first Jews returned from Babylon the walls of Jerusalem remained desolate and the people of God lived in affliction and shame.

It was at this juncture, in the year 445 B.C., that a man was raised up of God to match the need of the hour. Fourteen years after Ezra's return, God spoke to Nehemiah, prepared him for the task and called him to serve the Lord

in the rebuilding of the wall of Jerusalem. The opening
chapter of this book gives us the account of his preparation
and call, and of his purpose as he set about the task to which
God had called him.

Now these historical facts are only of secondary importance, but I believe them to be necessary in order that
we may understand the spiritual implications of this Book
of Nehemiah. I am not concerned primarily with a history
of the return here; I am concerned primarily that we
should draw from this book the immense spiritual lessons
that are here for us all.

There is a wall to be built around the city of your soul.
There is a wall to be built, a testimony to be erected around
your church. There is a wall of witness and testimony to be
built around the whole Kingdom of God in all the world.
Whether you be concerned primarily with building the
wall in your own soul, or with building the wall of your
church, or with building the wall of the Kingdom of God
throughout the whole world, you will discover that there
is no winning without warfare; there is no opportunity
without opposition; there is no victory without vigilance.
For whenever the people of God say, "Let us arise and
build," Satan says, "Let me arise and oppose."

I want to ask you first, therefore, to look at the preparation of Nehemiah for his task. He was in a high position in
the king's palace; we are told he was the king's cupbearer—
a place of real influence in court. Yet his interests were
not in the expansion of the Persian Empire; his concern
centered around God's purpose for His people in Jerusalem.

One day Nehemiah's brother and some other Jews returned from a brief visit to Jerusalem and reported to

Nehemiah the situation there. The story was a tragic one; it is given to us in the third verse of this chapter: "The remnant . . . are in great affliction and reproach; the wall of Jerusalem also is broken down and the gates thereof are burned with fire." It was one thing to know that state of affairs in a general way; it was quite another for his own brother to come and tell him the story and for Nehemiah to feel the pressure and burden of it in his own heart. The story of failure, set against his own knowledge of what was God's real purpose for the people in Jerusalem, changed this man's whole outlook on life. He knew what was God's intention; he became aware of how far short they had fallen from it, and with that knowledge and with that challenge before him, Nehemiah's whole outlook was transformed.

As he heard this story, we are told in the fourth verse that he sat down and he wept, and he mourned, and he fasted, and he prayed. But Nehemiah was not the last to weep over Jerusalem—one day our Lord sat on the slopes of Mt. Olivet and wept over that city, and mourned and prayed and sacrificed His life for it. And hundreds of people ever since have found that their life's work for God has only begun when they have wept and mourned and fasted and prayed over the revelation of conditions as they really are.

Let us learn this lesson from Nehemiah: you never lighten the load unless first you have felt the pressure in your own soul. You are never used of God to bring blessing until God has opened your eyes and made you see things as they are. There is no other preparation for Christian work than that. Nehemiah was called to build the wall, but first he had to weep over the ruins. You and I are supremely concerned about the walls I have mentioned: the wall in our own soul, the wall in our church, the wall of missionary enterprise. As you commence, by the grace of God, to rebuild the walls, you must first of all see the ruin in which they lie.

You cannot just slip into Christian work as a kind of hobby—you will fail terribly if you do. Before you attempt any service for God, I care not what it may be—how comparatively small, however much behind the scenes, however apparently insignificant—before you begin any service for the Master, I urge you first of all to survey the ruins around you.

I think first you should take a good, long look at the appalling lack of Christian teaching in our schools today before you start teaching a Sunday school class. Then you should take a long look at the failure concerning church observance, and at the vice which is openly encouraged. If you don't do what everybody else does, the world thinks you are crazy. Many disdain the work of God and think it is a mild form of insanity if you attend the place of worship. May I suggest that before you attempt any service for God, you get alone with God on your knees and mourn over the human heart.

Before you start any service for God, you should begin to mourn over the indifference of Christian people. Every church has a crowd around it. The Lord Jesus moved among the crowd, and He was moved with compassion because He saw them as sheep without a shepherd. Do crowds affect you like that when you see them moving through the streets? Do you have any concern for them? Ask God to give you that burden of soul.

Perhaps most of all as we survey the walls that need rebuilding, we are called upon to mourn over the failure of many of us to live lives which reflect Jesus Christ. Jerusalem's walls were in ruins and its gates were burned. To a modern city, of course, that means nothing; but God's purpose for Jerusalem was that its walls should be salvation and its gates should be praise, and the emblems of salvation and praise lay in utter ruin. Is God calling some of us to weep and mourn over the ruin of these emblems in our lives? The symbol of salvation, the symbol of praise, the wall that marks our separation from the world—does it today lie in tragic ruin?

There is no blessing until we look deep down in our own soul and see our spiritual life as it really is. Should you mourn over that in your life today? What about the wall of separation? What about the wall of your prayer life and your Bible study? What about the wall of your walk with God? What about the wall of your personal devotional life? What about the wall of your consistent testimony before others? What about the wall of your Christlike life? Do these things, in the sight of God, lie in ruins?

What about the wall of your church's testimony? What about the impact your fellowship is making upon your community today? We send our missionaries to Africa, to South America, to all the distant places of the world, and yet right on our doorstep there is often tragic, desperate need, with heathenism and revolt against God that apparently we can ignore.

It was after Nehemiah's weeping that he began working.

It was after his despair that there came determination. If we would mourn over the ruin that exists, we would find ourselves cast in utter dependence upon our God. That was Nehemiah's secret and that is the beginning of all Christian work. How much I pray that anybody who would do any form of service for the Master, not only for your sake but for the church's sake and for Christ's sake, that as such you have first sat down and wept over the ruins in your soul, in your church, and in the Kingdom of God. When God takes up a man and uses him in His service, the first thing He does is to show him his own utter inadequacy, insufficiency and unworthiness for the task. This was Nehemiah's preparation.

When we have a vision of ruin and brokenness and need, we are tempted to say, "We're helpless to do anything about it; we might as well never attempt it." Observe carefully, now, Nehemiah's prayer. Quite clearly, this was a man who had fed his soul on the Word of God. His prayer in this chapter is cast in the mold of God's revelation of Himself, and that kind of prayer can never fail. You will notice that Nehemiah sets the name of God on the one hand, and this man, the king of Persia, upon the other; for the first step in Nehemiah's task was that he must gain the favor of the king of Persia in order that he might take leave of absence to go to Jerusalem for the job to which God was calling him. This would be an impossible thing unless God intervened on his behalf, even though he had great influence in court and was in this position of responsibility.

Then Nehemiah moved in his prayer to confession; he included himself in the confession of the sins of his people, and in acknowledgment that they had not obeyed God, and that their troubles were the result of their own disobedience.

Notice also that this prayer was rooted in the past. Observe the tenth verse of this chapter: "These are thy servants and thy people, whom thou hast redeemed by thy great power, and by thy strong hand." In that prayer Nehemiah went back hundreds and hundreds of years, and he dared to remind God of the great deliverance from Egypt, the protection of the blood, the successful, triumphant journey into the land of blessing and victory; he dared to remind God of the covenant that God had given to His people, that some day they would possess this land. Nehemiah based all his prayer upon God's past dealings, and he saw in them a mirror of all God's future plans.

Whatever the ruin in your soul or mine may be; whatever may be the ruin of the impact of your church testimony; no matter how great the need may be on the vast mission fields of the world, where so many stations lie unoccupied; if only I can go back to God's past and ground my prayers upon a cross, upon the blood, upon an empty tomb, an ascended Lord, then I will see in these things the mirror reflecting all God's purposes for this world of ours.

We do not hear much of this kind of praying these days, I fear. Most of our prayers are just asking God to bless the work, and to bless some folks that are ill, and to keep us plugging along, to keep the work going. But prayer is not merely prattle, it is warfare. Real prayer engages in a battle. Real prayer is rooted in the promises of God and in the covenant of the blood. We have the reasons given to us by God in His Word why He should answer, and we can read them there. That is why Nehemiah's prayer was answered: it was based on God's purposes and God's promises.

Do you pray like that both in private and in public? We can look back to a place where Jesus died and shed His blood and rose from a tomb and ascended into heaven, and we can know He is coming again. Certainly He did not do all that to leave us living as we are today; or to leave our churches weak and inadequate in their impact and insufficient in their witness; or to leave the missionary situation in its tragic plight trying to confront the task of the world.

Take a long look at the cross and the blood flowing from His riven side, and then you will know something about this effective way of praying. Nehemiah's prayer was grounded in the Word, founded on the promises, rooted in God's past dealings.

But not only was this man prepared by vision and prepared by prayer; notice his determination of purpose. "Prosper thy servant this day," he said. And can you picture Nehemiah, prepared by prayer for all the things that confronted him that day, as he rose from his knees and took a deep breath and went into the presence of the king? He started the task. He had the ear of the king; he had obtained favor from the king; he had brilliant prospects that confronted him; but he shut himself away from all that, and like Moses of old, he chose ". . . rather to suffer affliction with the people of God, than to enjoy the pleasures of sin for a season" (Hebrews 11:25). This man, following that prayer which reassured him of God's intention and God's purpose for His people—this man, firm in his purpose, went out in the power of God and set about the task.

The principles of Christian service are just the same to-day. We are prepared to serve the Lord only by sacrifice. We are fit for the work of God only when we have wept over it, prayed about it, and then we are enabled by Him to tackle the job that needs to be done. May God give to us hearts that bleed, eyes that are wide open to see, minds that are clear to interpret God's purpose, wills that are obedient, and a determination that is utterly unflinching as we set about the tasks He would have us do.

2. Preparation and Equipment

And it came to pass in the month Nisan, in the twentieth year of Artaxerxes the king, that wine was before him: and I took up the wine, and gave it unto the king. Now I had not been beforetime sad in his presence.

Wherefore the king said unto me, Why is thy countenance sad, seeing thou art not sick? this is nothing else but sorrow of heart. Then I was very sore afraid,

And said unto the king, Let the king live for ever: why should not my countenance be sad, when the city, the place of my fathers' sepulchres, lieth waste, and the gates thereof are consumed with fire?

Then the king said unto me, For what dost thou make request? So I prayed to the God of heaven.

And I said unto the king, If it please the king, and if thy servant have found favour in thy sight, that thou wouldest send me unto Judah, unto the city of my fathers' sepulchres, that I may build it.

And the king said unto me, (the queen also sitting by him,) For how long shall thy journey be? and when wilt thou return? So it pleased the king to send me; and I set him a time.

Moreover I said unto the king, If it please the king, let letters be given me to the governors beyond the river, that they may convey me over till I come into Judah;

And a letter unto Asaph the keeper of the king's forest, that he may give me timber to make beams for the gates of the palace which appertained to the house, and for the wall of the city, and for the house that I shall enter into.

And the king granted me, according to the good hand of my God upon me.

Then I came to the governors beyond the river, and gave them the king's letters. Now the king had sent captains of the army and horsemen with me.

When Sanballat the Horonite, and Tobiah the servant, the Ammonite, heard of it, it grieved them exceedingly that there was come a man to seek the welfare of the children of Israel.

—Nehemiah 2:1-10

THE BURNT OFFERING is the Old Testament picture of entire consecration to the service of the Lord. The burnt offering was voluntary; it was *all* upon the altar; it was made by fire; it was a sweet savor unto the Lord.

I want to use the principle of the burnt offering to illustrate the message of Nehemiah 2:1-10, for this is the principle which not only lies behind the preparation and equipment of Nehemiah for God's service, but applies to every one of us in the service of the King of kings.

If I seem to major on minorities, on those that may be preparing themselves for the ministry, or for Christian or missionary work, I do not want the others to think they are excluded. In point of fact, I am deeply concerned that the principles of Christian service should be re-thought out in the presence of the Lord by every one of His people.

Let me bring you three thoughts from this portion of the Word. As the first of them, will you please observe with me the burden which Nehemiah carried.

A comparison between the first verse of chapter 1 and the corresponding verse of chapter 2 reveals that there had been a time lapse of some four months between the moment when Nehemiah learned of the sad condition of Jerusalem and the time when God opened the way for him to take action. The exact record of dates is not merely of historical interest. The moment Nehemiah knew the desperate need, the burden of it came intensely upon his spirit. He sat down, he wept, he mourned, he fasted, he prayed. But he carried that burden in secret until four months later the king, into whose presence Nehemiah had come every day, observed it for the first time and said, "Why is thy countenance sad, seeing thou art not sick? This is nothing else than sorrow of heart."

What had taken place in those four months is not told us, but we may well read between the lines. Nehemiah did not dash impetuously to the task the moment the need dawned upon him. He knew that before he could be successful in any work for God, he must have the favor of the king on the one hand, and he must be sure that God was calling him, on the other. How constantly in those four months Nehemiah must have sought the Lord alone, asking Him either to remove this burden altogether from his heart and spirit, or so to deepen it that it would be quite impossible for him to do other than respond.

How he must have pleaded with God concerning his position at court! It was hard enough to get into a Persian court; it was harder still to get out of it. To appear sad in the presence of the king was an unforgivable sin, punishable by death. Should he speak to the king and risk that? Or should he wait and trust God? After all, if God was calling him to do this work in Jerusalem, then God was surely able to work a miracle and give him favor in the presence of the king. So Nehemiah went on weeping and went on praying and went on fasting, until one day God opened the door. He didn't have to speak to the king at all; the king spoke to him.

The burden of his heart, the deep conviction lying so

heavily upon him, could no longer be hidden, and at the very moment when he found this crushing burden almost intolerable, God answered him. The initiative was not in Nehemiah's hands; it was in God's.

There is a very useful principle which we can draw from that story, a principle which is essential for every one of us to grasp in relation to our service for the Master. It is only the man with a crushing sense of burden and responsibility whom God can trust with His work. If you don't have a heart that is burdened with an overwhelming sense of conviction you will never be fruitful in the service of the Lord. The need never constitutes the call. How many people hear of appalling conditions in some distant land and immediately respond out of deep sympathy, and the result is disaster.

Our Lord said to His disciples, "Come unto me, all ye that are weary and heavy laden," but we relegate that invitation to the close of an evangelistic service instead of remembering that those words were spoken primarily to those who loved Him. If we are conscious of the multitude of needs in the service of God which would threaten to overburden and crush us—in our city and across this continent and throughout the world—to us, overwhelmed with that consciousness of need which none of us can individually meet, the Lord Jesus says, "Come unto me."

Recognition of need must be followed by earnest, persistent waiting upon God until the overwhelming sense of world need becomes a specific burden in my soul for one particular piece of work which God would have me do. Nobody should begin teaching children in the Sunday school, or preparing for the ministry, or training for the

mission field until, as the outcome of prayer, the burden
for the particular sphere of service has become so intense
that you cannot keep it alone any longer. When that happens, God acts. The initiative for opening doors of service
is never ours, but His.

Dent

His first preparation for all His servants is burden, and
when God sees we are willing to accept the burden, He
opens the door. If that principle were recognized there
would be far fewer resignations from church work when it
becomes difficult; there would be far fewer failures to stick
the pace of training for the ministry; there would be far
fewer collapses on the mission fields after only one term of
service; there would be far fewer attempts to push open the
door of service before you have revealed, when alone in
the presence of God, that you are willing to bear the burden.
". . . neither will I offer burnt offerings unto the Lord my
God of that which doth cost me nothing," said David; and
before I venture upon any task for my Lord, I want to pay
the price of real travail within my own soul, and to know
the crushing load of a burden that I can carry no longer.
When God sees I have that, He will open the door. And
God help the children whom any Sunday school teacher
professes to teach who has never felt that load upon his or
her heart.

Not only was there a burden that Nehemiah carried, but
a blessing that Nehemiah coveted. ". . . if thy servant have
found favour in thy sight, that thou wouldest send me unto
Judah, unto the city of my fathers' sepulchres, that I may
build it" (v. 5). Nehemiah wanted to know that he had been
sent. ". . . let letters be given me to the governors beyond
the river," requested Nehemiah in verse 7, "that they may

convey me over till I came into Judah." He wanted to know that he would be safe. "And a letter unto Asaph the keeper of the king's forest, that he may give me timber . . . for the gates . . . and for the wall . . . and for the house. . . ." Nehemiah wanted to know that he would be supplied.

Was he asking too much? What about the life of faith? Was Nehemiah asking for too much here? Certainly not! The king was well able to give him all he asked, and all of these things were absolutely essential if this task once begun was to be completed. Was it not an immense source of strength as he began to rebuild the walls of Jerusalem and as he faced all the increasing opposition and discouragement, to look back upon that interview in the presence of the king, and to remember his commissioning and the promised supply of every need? The fact that the good hand of God had been upon him then assured him for all the future days of his ministry. Here again, my friends, is a vital lesson for us all. Sent, safe, supplied—all those factors are supremely important in any service for God.

The dominating factor in all our service for the Master is not the need of other people, but the command of the Lord Jesus Christ—His absolute sovereignty, His right to send His people anywhere, His right to order our steps as well as order our stops. If that principle is forgotten, the needs are so great and the conditions are so perplexing that we shall certainly falter in our service. A missionary is someone who is sent by the Lord, as He Himself was sent by the Father: ". . . as my Father hath sent me, even so send I you." Consequently, the true source of inspiration for service is always behind me and never in front of me. The challenge will always be in front of me; as will the means.

FIRST UNITED PRESBYTERIAN CHURCH
2619 BROADWAY
OAKLAND 12, CALIFORNIA

But the power and the motive of all Christian work is never what I see ahead, but is that indescribable, undefinable pressure of the Holy Spirit that has put me there. It is only that, dear Christian, which will keep your hand upon the plough when the going is hard. It is only such conviction that will give "stickability" at the task. To be in any service for God, and to lack the assurance of being called and sent, is tragedy indeed.

I believe the "show business" which is so incorporated into so much Christian work today is causing the church to drift far from the conception of our Lord concerning discipleship. It seems to be instilled in us that we have to do something exceptional for God as a sort of token, as an example of courage and of sacrifice at which everybody will gaze, openmouthed, and say, "What a wonderful man!" You do not need the grace of God for that. Human nature and human pride will take us through many a crisis in life, and make us do what seems to be the big thing in leaving our home and offering ourselves for Christian service. "My, what a man," says the world. That requires no grace; it appeals to the flesh. But I want to say to you from the depths of my heart that it needs all the grace of God to go through drudgery and poverty, to live an ignored existence as a saint, unnoticed by anybody. For if this commission is behind us in Christian work, remember, always we are sent out to be exceptional in ordinary things, among sometimes mean people, in frequently sordid surroundings. Only the man sent by the King of kings could take that, and only the man with a true burden will ever accept it.

After three years of intimate fellowship with Jesus Christ, all the disciples forsook Him and fled. They came to the end of themselves and their self-sufficiency, and they realized that if ever they were to be any different, it must be by receiving a different spirit altogether, and Jesus breathed upon them and said, ". . . as my Father hath sent me, even so send I you . . . Receive ye the Holy Ghost." Have you been sent to the work that you are doing for God today? If you haven't, the sooner you quit, the better.

Nehemiah did not only want to know that he was sent, he wanted to be kept safe. Have I the right to ask to be kept safe in the Master's work? Certainly not in a physical sense —we are called upon to hazard our lives for the gospel if need be. The sentence of death, as it was in Paul, will often be in the true servant of God. But we are entitled to be kept safe in the spiritual sense. Nehemiah, you observe, had men who went with him on the journey to protect him. Nobody should ever go to the field for God, or to any service for God, alone. He must have those who will pray, who are with him in spirit at his side constantly, for the man who goes in answer to God's call will face many shattering disillusionments. He will be subjected to perils he has never before experienced. He will be submitted to temptations hitherto unknown. He will have to face loneliness that he had never imagined, and homesickness from which he thought he was delivered when he was a little boy at school. But that man who has left everything in life which he might hold dear is entitled to spiritual protection and to expect it from men who know how to pray and to write, and above all who know how to enter into his needs and share them at the throne of grace. Once a missionary leaves the shores of this country, and has had his valedictory, he is often forgotten, unfortunately.

You may never sail from America across the seas in God's service, but you may, every one of you, be the instrument in God's hands in keeping some beloved missionary safe from spiritual loneliness and spiritual depression, because he knows that he is in your heart always. It is because so many fail at home that so many fail on the field and come back casualties.

Then Nehemiah wanted to be sure of supplies. Of course, there are some people who believe that all that is necessary for missionary preparation and safety is simply to drop the unfortunate missionary somewhere by parachute into a jungle in Africa and leave him there, piously saying "God will supply all your need." Very nice, if you're at the right end of the parachute. Faith—do you call that faith? No, my friend, I'm sorry, but I believe it is sheer murder. Do you have some share in the keeping of some missionary upon the field? Do you give of your substance? Do you send food and clothing, medical equipment and other things of which so many are in need? This is a world-wide enterprise in which every Christian is called to share.

But rebuilding for God demands much more than material supplies; it demands spiritual resources. Are you being supplied there today in the work that you are doing? Is God meeting your need? Have you got what is required for the job that you're in? "But unto every one of us," says the Apostle, writing to the Ephesians, "is given grace according to the measure of the gift of Christ." Yes, He promises grace for everything that is within His will for you, but for nothing that is outside His will for you.

If you are teaching a class in Sunday school, it is not only ability to teach that matters, it is the spirit that you impart

through teaching. Are you being supplied? If you are studying for the ministry, it is not only the ability to learn the
Bible as a textbook and repeat a thousand texts by memory,
it is the grace to proclaim the Word of God in the power of
the Holy Spirit. Are you being supplied right now? Or are
you living at such tension and strain and at the end of yourself that it is quite evident, if you would only stop and think,
that you are out of the will of God altogether? To be sent,
to be kept in safety, to be supplied before I will venture out
into the service of the Master, whatever it may be, I must
know that I am going into it because God has sent me; I must
know that I am safe in it because I have people praying for
me; I must know that I am being supplied now in the work
I am doing *here* by His grace, for if I do not know how to
draw upon spiritual resources now, I shall never learn how
to do it in circumstances that are utterly different.

In the last place, not only do I want you to think about
the burden Nehemiah carried and the blessing that he coveted, I want you to think with me about the battle which
he caused. ". . . it grieved them exceedingly that there was
come a man to seek the welfare of the children of Israel"
(v. 10). We shall meet Sanballat and Tobiah again another
time; all I want you to observe now is that they knew
perfectly well what Nehemiah was after. He was concerned about the welfare of the children of Israel; he was
a man with no other motive than that. He had no axe to
grind, no selfish interests, no vain ambitions, no desire for
personal glory; therefore he was a marked man. And as soon
as such a man says, "Let us arise and build," the enemy says,
"Let us arise and stop him." It was this man who caused the
battle to begin. It was this man who drew the fire of the

enemy to himself. It was this man who aroused the enmity of Sanballat and Tobiah.

There were plenty of other Jews in Jerusalem, and they'd been there a long time, but they had no concern for a broken-down wall and a ruined testimony. They were perfectly satisfied with things as they were going; they never thought it to be a reproach to the name of God; they were no menace to the devil. But Nehemiah was a man with a burden, who had been sent and supplied, a man with vision and vocation. Here was a man whose whole attitude was a declaration of war against things as they were. And as the enemy saw his determination to retrieve ground that was lost, at once they were aroused to oppose.

There is no battle anywhere in the spiritual sense until the Christian pitches in. There is no concern in the mind of Satan about the church at all until he sees a selfless Christian seeking only the glory of God, determined to challenge the Satanic grip upon men's hearts and lives in the name of the Lord. Does your service for God cause Satan any worry at all? How much overtime has the devil to do in hell because of your church? I can answer that question by asking you some others: Are you interested in anything save the welfare of the people? Have you any ambition except to please God? Have you concern for any reputation but the Master's? Then, and only then, is Satan angry.

Those are hard questions which I have already had to face on my knees alone with God concerning my own life, and I invite you in the name of the Lord to do the same. ". . . neither will I offer burnt offerings unto the Lord my God of that which doth cost me nothing." I know what I am

talking about when I say that the costliest preparation of
all is to look into the face of the Lord Jesus alone, with no
applause and no public, and to say to Him, "Lord Jesus
Christ, in this task I seek only Thy glory and the blessing
of souls."

Have I painted a rugged picture for you? Well, my
friend, it is a rugged task, you know. And if anybody is to
undertake Christian work in my church, I am determined
that they should know at the outset what is involved, and
then they will never be able to blame me for ignorance.
Some may resign because the price is to great too pay, but
a hundred people with a burden are better than a thousand
without. It is quality and not quantity that God is looking
for; this is an age of mass production, but in the spiritual
sense God deals with men one by one.

3. Facing the Challenge

So I came to Jerusalem, and was there three days.

And I arose in the night, I and some few men with me; neither told I any man what my God had put in my heart to do at Jerusalem: neither was there any beast with me, save the beast that I rode upon.

And I went out by night by the gate of the valley, even before the dragon well, and to the dung port, and viewed the walls of Jerusalem, which were broken down, and the gates thereof were consumed with fire.

Then I went on to the gate of the fountain, and to the king's pool: but there was no place for the beast that was under me to pass.

Then went I up in the night by the brook, and viewed the wall, and turned back, and entered by the gate of the valley, and so returned.

And the rulers knew not whither I went, or what I did; neither had I as yet told it to the Jews, nor to the priests, nor to the nobles, nor to the rulers, nor to the rest that did the work.

Then said I unto them, Ye see the distress that we are in, how Jerusalem lieth waste, and the gates thereof are burned with fire: come, and let us build up the wall of Jerusalem, that we be no more a reproach.

Then I told them of the hand of my God which was good upon me; as also the king's words that he had spoken unto me. And they said, Let us rise up and build. So they strengthened their hands for this good work.

But when Sanballat the Horonite, and Tobiah the serv-

ant, the Ammonite, and Geshem the Arabian, heard it, they laughed us to scorn, and despised us, and said, What is this thing that ye do? will ye rebel against the king?

Then answered I them, and said unto them, The God of heaven, he will prosper us; therefore we his servants will arise and build: but ye have no portion, nor right, nor memorial, in Jerusalem.

—Nehemiah 2:11-20

THE SECOND CHAPTER of the Book of Nehemiah reveals some essential principles for Christian service. Nehemiah had been sent and supplied by the king; he had taken a three-months' journey and arrived at Jerusalem, there to face the challenge of the task which God had allotted to him. What an insight there is in these verses into this man's Christian character and godliness of life! What an insight there is into methods that are essential to the success of all Christian work! But we do not come to the Bible primarily to study a man's character or Christian methods, we come to meet God; a message has little value unless it brings us to the feet of our Saviour.

I want you to observe that there are three essentials to Christian service that are clearly defined in these verses, so we will turn the searchlight of this passage upon our work for God. Is it effectual? Is it spiritual? Or are we dissatisfied with it? Is it getting rather stale? Is it accomplishing nothing in spite of all our efforts? If so, let us ask ourselves, and ask the Holy Spirit to teach us, if the reason may be that one of the three essentials of Christian service is missing in our work for the Lord—at least, if not entirely, in part?

There is a first essential that I will call *investigation.* Before Nehemiah began, he was determined to know the worst. We see him in these verses as a man with the counsel of God in his heart, conferring not with flesh and blood, for he told no man what God had put in his heart to do. He had a secret place in his soul which he had reserved for his God and himself. It is good to have Christian friends, but it is dangerous to wear your heart on your sleeve. Have a secret place somewhere which nobody knows anything about but you and God.

Here was a man who was a born leader; here was a man who was resolute, reserved; here was a man who was in no hurry. Nehemiah tarried three days at Jerusalem before he even began to investigate. He did not start his service for God until, alone with God, he had counted the cost. But once he had put his hand upon the plough, he would never look back, nor take his hand off until he was able to say, "It is finished."

Nehemiah took a tour of inspection on horseback at nighttime; he went around the city, going out the valley gate, taking a tour around the walls and returning at the same entrance. In places so great was the ruin and devastation that he had to dismount from his horse and stumble over the wreckage himself. But in the course of that night, while others slept, Nehemiah—wide-awake, burdened, conscious of desperate need and shame and ruin all around him—diagnosed the situation, surveyed the ruined walls, and contemplated the magnitude of the task to which God had called him.

Imagine his grief of heart as he stumbled among those ruins of what was once a great and mighty fortress! Whenever a real work of God is to be done—a real work, not something superficial, but real—some faithful, burdened servant has to take a journey such as Nehemiah took, to weep in the night over the ruins, to wrestle in some dark

Gethsemane in prayer. It is utter folly to refuse to believe that things are as bad as they really are. It is vital in any undertaking for God to know the worst, for whenever there is to be a wonderful movement of the Holy Spirit, it begins with someone like Nehemiah who was bold enough to look at facts, to diagnose them, and then to rise to the task.

Are our hearts ever stirred like that? Have you ever lost one hour of sleep over the tragic spiritual dearth of your church and your city? Has it ever kept you awake? And have you cried, "O God, what can I do about this thing?" Do you ever care that multitudes of people in our own land are as ignorant of the truth of the gospel as the unevangelized heathen in Brazil or Africa? Do you care that over fifteen hundred million people are without Christ today? Do you care that thirty million people die every year, that every time the second hand of the clock moves, a soul is going out into eternity? Are those just statistics, or do they make your heart bleed?

There was a great American soul-winner by the name of Samuel Hadley, who, one night in New York after he had been visiting in just a few of that great city's homes, leaned against a lamppost and was heard by someone to groan and say, "O God, the sin of the city is breaking my heart."

Think of the coldness of our prayers. Think of the mere routine of our service that takes up so much of our time that we haven't time to stop and ask God what He wants us to do. Think of the carelessness of our own Christian walk. Think of the poverty of our witness, the compromise of our lives. Before God will ever do a work of revival, He will break our hearts; do you know that? You may have thought that to weep over a world in collapse, and over the sin in our own lives would leave you in utter despair, but it will not. It was into Nehemiah's broken heart that God put the knowledge of what to do with Jerusalem. The immense need of any work for God can always be met by the infinite grace and power of our Saviour. Students for the Christian ministry, workers and laborers for the gospel, never shirk a thorough investigation of the facts. Do not enter into service until you have counted the cost.

However, when you have sensed the need, felt the burden in your heart, and counted the cost, remember that the God who called you is sufficient for every emergency, and then go right through. Never look back or take your hand off the plough for one day until you can look your Lord in the face and say, "I have finished the work which Thou gavest me to do."

The second word that seems the key to this passage is cooperation. In verse 17, Nehemiah, having faced the magnitude of the task, realized the absolute necessity of securing other people to help him. ". . . come, and let us build . . . that we be no more a reproach." The fact that the city which had once been the center of God's dealings with His people lay in ruins was not merely a reproach to them, it was a reproach to the honor and to the name of their God. That was to be the inspiration and the power behind all this work of revival. It was not simply a disgrace to them, it was a shame to Him. The people worshiped the same God; therefore they would share the same work. Unity of vision must mean unity of purpose.

If you will glance over the third chapter of Nehemiah you will see how effectively and efficiently Nehemiah planned his work. I'm so glad that by the grace of God you and I may ask that our lives be marked not only by spirituality but by efficiency. It should not be true that a Christian simply blunders his way through; he should work to a planned strategy. Nehemiah divided the work among forty-two groups; he did not believe in a one-man ministry! Neither do I. Oh, yes, there must be leadership, but every one of the Lord's people must have a part in the Lord's work.

All along the wall the people worked, their one desire to see it completed. Each group was united in determination to finish the particular task allotted to them. They were not jealous of what somebody else was doing; nor were they concerned about that job or this, for God had given them a portion to do in the rebuilding of the wall, and they set themselves to the task with all might and main. And all those groups were united to each other. How thrilling! They were all conscious of their next-door neighbors, and thankful for their cooperation; they were all working together as one around that wall. There was no separation; there was no in-dependent spirit. Because they were one in vision, they were one in purpose.

S. D. Gordon said, "Cooperation increases efficiency in amazing proportions. Two working together in perfect agreement have fivefold the efficiency of the same two working separately." The old Book says that where one can handle a thousand, two can dispose of ten thousand. This is as true in prayer as it is in action. "A united church," said S. D. Gordon, "would be an unconquerable church. But the moment cooperation is sacrificed as an essential, real power

is at the disappearing point." A crew working together for
God alone—*that* is cooperation.

It is important to remember that all who are Christians
have one life. In the sight of heaven there is only one life that
matters before God—it is the life of the Lord Jesus, indwelling each one of us by His Spirit. This is an amazing
fellowship. Because we share that one life, we share one
great purpose and one great work: it is the building of
lives into the Kingdom of God, and in such a task one
hundred per cent cooperation between Christian people is
absolutely vital. The greatest menace to revival is the
Christian who refuses to work with other people because his
views differ on certain matters of Biblical interpretation
which are nonessential in relation to evangelism.

It is interesting to note that Nehemiah set each group to
work on that part of the wall which was nearest to where
that group member lived. I must emphasize that our first
obligation for Christ is always our own neighborhood.
Wouldn't the bells of heaven ring today if every believer
would say this before God, "Lord, I will make my own immediate locality my mission field. I will see to it that every
family is regularly supplied with gospel literature and urged
to attend church"?

You see, my friends, in Christian work organizing and
agonizing should go together. Alas, too often organizing
has crowded out agonizing. There is too much working
before men and too little waiting before God. There is
more and more motion and less and less unction. We wrestle
with problems in endless committees and conferences, but
we seldom wrestle on our knees against our real enemy,
Satan. Many a committee, of course, has a fine program,

but how many have a real spiritual burden? Oh, may God give each of us that burden in order that there may be the one hundred per cent cooperation in this work! We have no room here for the independent Christian; we are engaged in one supreme task, that of reaching this world for God, and it will take all of us.

Another word here: the principles of Christian work are first, investigation; second, cooperation; and <u>third, *determination.*</u>

In verses 19 and 20 you notice that Nehemiah is just about to run into trouble: Sanballat, Tobiah and Geshem. They have a great variety of tactics, these three, and we shall be examining their tactics later on. Meanwhile, I want you to observe the courageous way in which Nehemiah dealt with them at the very first onslaught as they heaped scorn upon him. "But when Sanballat the Horonite, and Tobiah the servant, the Ammonite, and Geshem the Arabian, heard it, they laughed us to scorn, and despised us, and said, What is this thing that ye do? will ye rebel against the king? Then answered I them, and said unto them, The God of heaven, he will prosper us; therefore we his servants will arise and build: but ye have no portion, nor right, nor memorial, in Jerusalem."

He tells the truth about God to begin with; he could point to the good hand of God upon him and declare that the God of heaven would prosper him in the work. After all, it was God's work, and He was with it and in it. He told the truth about himself and his workers: they were doing the Lord's business, and say what the enemy might and do what the enemy could, they were going to carry out the work. He told the truth about the enemy: "You've got no portion and no right in Jerusalem; there is nothing that belongs to you here. You've no right to the privileges of this place; you've no part in it. And when the wall is built, you'll be built outside it, anyway, so get out." Nehemiah spoke with courage and boldness and authority to the enemy.

There is no message which does not bring us to the feet of the Lord Jesus Christ. Here is a man called to the service of God and here are three great essentials for Christian work and Christian service: investigate, cooperate, determine.

The same qualities which were exercised by Nehemiah in rebuilding that wall were exercised by the Lord Jesus Christ in saving your soul. The Saviour has undertaken the saving of lives that have been marred by sin. If the cross means anything at all, it means the sentence of shame and of judgment upon human nature; by His death the Lord Jesus Christ has made it possible for poor, helpless, sinful people like us to stand before God complete, without a trace of guilt. How? First, by *investigation*.

Tell me this—has the Lord ever looked into your heart? He looked Peter through and through; He searched out the rich young ruler and scores of others. Have you ever allowed Jesus to diagnose your case? It is amazing how we Christians can hide behind our creed and our doctrine and our belief in the Bible and allow ourselves to become hard and cynical so that the task that should be so tender has become cankerous. Are you living like that? Does the Lord ever search you? I want Him to hold you and me in His searching gaze and investigate our lives. I know I shall never see the blessing through my ministry for which my heart longs unless I am prepared to ask Him to show me the worst. Have you ever done that? What about the crowd? What about your relatives and neighbors? What about your life in private, most of all?

Somehow in my heart I would be conscious of the Holy Spirit investigating my character, my spirit, my belief. I want to hear the still, small voice saying to me, "My child, come, let us arise together and build, that we be no more a reproach." That *we* be no more a reproach; that He and I, that He and you be no more a reproach. Oh, how I pray that God's Spirit may speak to your heart like that. "Come, my child, you and I together—" you and the Lord. "Let us arise and build, that we be no more a reproach." Oh, what a reproach your life is and my life is—are they not?

Tell me, in the light of the cross, isn't it a scandal that you and I live today as we do? We have so little burden and so little concern—I know I do. The things we think about, the things we covet, and the things that grip our hearts and lives, are so unworthy. But Jesus says to you, "Come, let us build together." He can do nothing for you if you are not willing. It isn't a question of my ability to rebuild this life, or the wall that has broken down. It isn't a question of my state or the state of the ruins; God's Spirit can deal with all that. It is my willingness. "Ye will not come to me, that ye might have life," says the Master. This is not will-power but grace-power.

There is one kind of person for whom God can do nothing; it is the person who is absolutely satisfied with what he is at this moment in the sight of God. There are many who say, "We are rich and increased with goods, and have need of nothing," when in reality you are "blind, and miserable and naked and poor and destitute and beggars," and in desperate need, as God has spoken to us. Oh, if there is someone saying, "I don't know what you are talking about. We're getting along splendidly"—my friend, let God speak to your heart today and investigate things as they are in your life.

The next word is _cooperation._ Does He have my willingness to be at His disposal? I tell you, He will never rest until He has perfected all that concerns your life and mine. He has counted the cost, and He will not cease until the work is done. This is His purpose: "I will," He said, "that they also, whom thou hast given me, be with me where I am. . . ." That is God's purpose. And if there is one yielded life in which Jesus Christ lives, and that life were ultimately lost, all the honor of God would be destroyed. The yielded, surrendered, committed, dedicated, consecrated life is as safe for time and eternity as God's faithfulness and God's Book and God's promise.

In the building of the new Jerusalem, of that home that Jesus has gone to prepare for us, are you being built in or out of it? "I am the door," said Jesus; "by me if any man enter in, he shall be saved, and shall go in and out, and find pasture" (John 10:9). That is heaven's door, the door that the heart of the Lord Jesus opens, "I am the door," He says. But there is another, "Behold, I stand at the door, and knock: if any man hear my voice, and open the door, I will come in . . ." (Revelation 3:20). If I keep that door shut, one day the door of God's heart will be shut to me.

Investigation . . . cooperation . . . determination. The Lord Jesus Christ set His heart with those principles, and upon them built your salvation and mine. And because He did that, and has investigated our lives, and tested the willingness of our surrender, we are determined to please God.

I trust that those same principles by which the Lord Jesus saves and keeps may be the principles which govern all your service, your ministry, and your testimony for Him.

4. The Starting Point for All

And next unto them repaired Jedaiah the son of Harumaph, even over against his house. And next unto him repaired Hattush the son of Hashabniah.

After him repaired Benjamin and Hashub over against their house. After him repaired Azariah the son of Maaseiah the son of Ananiah by his house.

After them repaired Zadok the son of Immer over against his house. After him repaired also Shemaiah the son of Shechaniah, the keeper of the east gate

After him repaired Hananiah the son of Shelemiah, and Hanun the sixth son of Zalaph, another piece. After him repaired Meshullam the son of Berechiah over against his chamber.

—Nehemiah 3:10, 23, 29, 30

THIS PASSAGE FROM the New Testament is a commentary on Nehemiah, chapter three: "For other foundation can no man lay than that is laid, which is Jesus Christ. Now if any man build upon this foundation gold, silver, precious stones, wood, hay, stubble; Every man's work shall be made manifest: for the day shall declare it, because it shall be revealed by fire; and the fire shall try every man's work of what sort it is" (I Corinthians 3:11-13).

This chapter of Nehemiah is the remarkable record of the rebuilding of the wall around Jerusalem. The entire population responded to Nehemiah's plea for help and cooperation, and this account shows a warmhearted and enthusiastic spirit. Each had his own particular job to do, and no one was envious of the job that somebody else did. Each was satisfied with his particular assignment, and every section of the wall was cared for.

Beginning at the sheep gate of Jerusalem, these verses take us on a tour clockwise from the west to north to east and back again south to the sheep gate. If you took that tour in your imagination, you would see every man at his appointed task; there were no shirkers and no grumblers. All were united in their objective: to get the wall completed. How irresistible a church would be with an army of workers like that! It is for oneness of objective and happiness in the task allotted to us, with absence of friction and discontent, that we must ever work and pray.

Our attention is especially drawn to a phrase which occurs four times in this chapter: ". . . he repaired . . . over against his house." That is where every real work for God must begin—at home. That is a principle throughout the whole revelation of the Book. The disciples were to commence at Jerusalem, the place where they had failed and denied their Lord. There must be victory in the place of past failure before the doors will ever open to spheres of wider service. The witness of Christian people is no more effective anywhere in public than it is at home. Here, then, is the starting place for all of us. A church is no stronger than its homes, for a church is made up of families. As we pray for God to bring revival to our churches, I want you to think of it here in terms of homes.

What a wonderful word "home" is! Here are the most sacred and intimate associations of life. Here joys and sorrows are shared. Here God's faithfulness is proved and His blessing experienced. But, alas, the sanctity of all these things is so often lost and many of our homes today are in great need of spiritual rebuilding. Here's where we must begin if we mean business with God, upon the only foundation that can ever be laid—the foundation of Christ.

As we examine this record of those who repaired near their own houses, we are impressed with the significance of their names. In the Hebrew tongue, a man's name was often descriptive of his character. That was true of God, also. The name of God always reveals the character of God, and in the Old Tetsament as one name after another was given to Deity, it only served to express just another aspect of His character. It was also true of individuals; true of Moses; true of Joshua, "the saviour"; true of Jacob, "the supplanter"; every name had immense significance in relation to the character of the person.

Let us look, then, at the names of these four who "repaired against their house." As we do so, I trust that the Holy Spirit may speak to us and reveal to us that home is the place where we must begin if we would know the blessing of God. Verse 10 says, "And next unto them repaired Jedaiah . . . even over against his house. . . ." This man's name means "invoker of God." He was a man who knew how to pray, a man whose life was founded upon prayer.

Let me ask you, has the wall of prayer broken down in your home? I want to speak to you very simply here, very lovingly, very practically. Does the wall of your family prayer life lie in ruins? Or is there a cherished moment every day when you and your loved ones gather around God's Word and kneel together in prayer? Did you begin your home as husband and wife like that, but now you are too busy, too tired, too rushed to pray? Maybe you have come to the place where you say, "It doesn't matter." Is your home no longer the place of harmony it used to be, no longer sweet and gracious and tender? Now, alas, there are often harsh words and short tempers. That is not home as it once was. Of course, your children have probably noticed, and they have become careless about spiritual things too.

Oh, how desperately the wall of prayer needs to be rebuilt in your home! See the ruin it is in; see the reproach that it is. Perhaps you are a pillar in your church, you are looked up to with respect as you serve in the church of God. For you are an active Christian worker—but that's the tragedy: an active Christian worker has replaced a loving Christian father or mother. You're too busy, much too busy. Begin again today to be an invoker of God. Re-establish the family altar and repair the broken-down wall of prayer.

In verse 23 of this chapter we read: "After him repaired Benjamin and Hashub over against their house. . . ." Hashub merely means "associate," so here we are going to concentrate a moment on Benjamin, whose name means "the son of my right hand," the one who is there to protect me. Is the wall of protection in your home broken down? What is it that keeps a home safe? All the insurance policies in the world cannot achieve that, and there are far worse enemies to our homes that can invade their security than mere burglars. You remember that the blessing of God given to Benjamin was, "The beloved of the Lord shall dwell in safety by him; and the Lord shall cover him all the day long, and he shall dwell between his shoulders" (Deuteronomy 33:12). What wonderful protection is that! How precious is that home where the husband and wife dwell between the shoulders of the Almighty, where they are kept in safety by Him! Such is the blessing which only the presence and power of the Lord Jesus brings to our home, where He is sovereign, where His will is done, where every member of the family "seeks first the kingdom of God and his righteousness." In such a home there is absolute protection—not necessarily from illness, poverty, pain, or death—but *always* from worry, from fear and from friction. Those who dwell between the shoulders of the Almighty, and who know His protection, are able to say, not merely as one of the verses they learned in childhood but as a truth learned from the warp and woof of their experience: ". . . all things work together for good to them that love God . . ." (Romans 8:28).

But what if in your home the wall of that protection has broken down? You have not sought first His Kingdom and His righteousness; you have not committed your home to His protection, and somehow over the years serious dis-integration has set in. Perhaps, quite frankly, you have begun to wonder how much longer your home and family life will be able to hold together. How urgently you need to face the ruin of a disintegrated home! I would remind you that "He is able to keep that which I have committed unto Him against that day," but He will *only* keep what I have committed. Maybe there are assets of your home life that have never been committed, and because they are not committed, they have not been kept. Benjamin dwelt in safety by the Lord, between His shoulders. Is your home like that?

In verse 29 of this chapter we read: "After them repaired Zadok the son of Immer over against his house. . . ." And Zadok means "justice." Tell me, is the wall of integrity broken down in your home? Do you remember those mar-riage vows you made to love, to cherish, to honor, to keep yourselves only unto each other until death parts you? Have you been faithful? Do you long for the company of your dear one more than anybody else in the world? Or is there someone whom you value more, of whom you say, "This person is more sympathetic than my wife (or husband)"?

The sacred wall of integrity must be restored if there is to be blessing in your home.

The grim facts are that thousands of even so-called Christian homes are only held together for the sake of appearances. Where once there was such love and such mutual devotion, now all is cold and unloving. The broken wall of integrity ruins not only your personal testimony, but it is also a blight upon the whole witness of the church. How precious is the home where there are no secrets, where there is complete trust and confidence and respect!

Notice that Zadok was the son of Immer—his name means "talkative." Do you know of any weapon that does more harm in a home than the tongue? Certain things should mark a Christian home in this respect. There are some secrets that husband and wife should share only with God. I wonder if the wall of integrity in some homes is broken down because of gossip. Not only is the relationship of husband and wife and children sacred, however, but also the relationship of that home with the church. In a real Christian home the father and mother will not criticize the preacher in front of their children. And if he is deserving of criticism (as most of us are), they will pray rather than criticize. In a God-honoring home, fellow Christians are not maligned, either. Has the integrity of that relationship been preserved in your home? In the true Christian home the church is never pulled to pieces; other members of the Christian family are never pulled to pieces, either. Maybe God is speaking to you now because you have been careless and flippant, critical and gossipy, unkind in your speech concerning either the preacher or the church or your fellow Christians. Let the Spirit of God search you out. That is the kind of thing that blocks revival, did you know that? Perhaps God is speaking to you about building up the wall of integrity again.

Then in the thirtieth verse of this chapter I read, ". . . After him repaired Meshullam the son of Berechiah over against his chamber." Now there is something about this man that appeals to me very much, because it may be that the kind of thing I have been talking about does not quite apply to you. But it may get you just here, because apparently this Meshullam lived in a one-room apartment alone, "his chamber." He felt insignificant, perhaps, and a very little part of the work was allotted to him; it almost seemed that it was not worth bothering about, that it did not count. But this man's name, Meshullam, means "devoted." And he is the son of Berechiah; his father's name means "the Lord hath blessed him." The blessing of the Lord in a home does not depend upon whether it is big or little. "The blessing of the Lord, it maketh rich . . ." in a deeper sense than that, and it "addeth no sorrow" (Proverbs 10:22).

Just a humble little apartment was home for Meshullam, but his life speaks of an utter, absolute dedication. Perhaps he was content to have his home so small because he lived on such a sacrificial level. Perhaps he was so devoted to the Lord that his home was just an instrument, a place in which to sleep and eat and pray, that was all.

Tell me, is the wall of devotion and dedication to Christ broken down in your home? Perhaps there used to be a sacrificial service for Christ; perhaps others used to come into your little one-room apartment and talk with you about the Saviour. You would never miss the church prayer meeting; you would never fail to speak to your neighbors about the Lord Jesus. But now you are irregular in your worship and your service has slipped.

Perhaps your home, instead of being an instrument of blessing, has become an idol. You live for its amenities, its gifts, and its equipment. You live for its furniture, for its carpets; these things fill your mind. And the wall of prayer, the wall of protection, the wall of purity, the wall of passionate devotion to Jesus is broken. Is that true?

God looks down upon His family and He sees homes where the wall of prayer is in ruins, or the wall of protection gone and the home disintegrating; or the wall of purity broken; or the wall of passionate devotion to Himself neglected.

"I'm too small," you say. "It doesn't matter about me; I don't count." Oh yes, you do! The wall is continuous, and if there is a gap in it anywhere, the enemy will break through. If there are gaps in the ranks the whole testimony of the church is affected. You cannot expect the blessing of God upon your home if you criticize your neighbor and gossip concerning the preacher and pull to pieces the church and the people who worship in it. Oh, the wall of integrity that needs to be rebuilt between church and home and family in so many places!

What is that going to mean? Well, perhaps it means for someone, some husband or wife, you are going to look at each other and say, "We haven't prayed; the family altar is broken. Before we have another meal we are going to kneel together and acknowledge it, and we are going to commit our home to Christ." The wall is going to be repaired.

Perhaps someone is going to have to look into the face of his wife, or the wife into the face of her husband and confess, "I haven't been faithful. I haven't been true, and I acknowledge it. I confess it before you and before God." The wall of integrity is going to be rebuilt.

Perhaps there are fathers and mothers who have been speaking lightly and carelessly concerning neighbors and church and fellow Christians, and they are going to have to sit down with their children and say, "We've been wrong. We've talked lightly, and we have been critical and unkind."

My home was not, as I understand it now, a Christian home, but I can never forget one day—it made a mark in my memory. There had been hard words in the home which I had overheard as a child, and I was amazed. For two or three days there was a strange coldness between my father and my mother. Then one Sunday midday my father looked across the table to my mother and said, "I'm so sorry that I've spoken to you as I have. I'm ashamed of myself." I was not a Christian, but I remember going back to my room after that meal and kneeling down and saying, "O God, thank you for a father like that. Make me like him." Parents who are prepared to humble themselves will gain the love and gratitude of their children.

Maybe it means that you will give your home utterly to Christ and will ask Him once again that it may not be an idol, but rather an instrument of blessing to others.

But it may be that someone is not even upon the right foundation at all, that what I've been saying you have known to be right and, alas, only too true in your home, but the trouble with you is that yours is not a Christian home. My friend, for you to try to build a wall without a foundation would mean that the wall would only fall down again. If you are determined that you are going to be right with your wife and family, and that you will in the future pray and read your Bibles together, and that your marriage relationship will be restored, then I can tell you frankly that before the week is out the wall that you started to rebuild will have collapsed. The only thing for you to do is to step onto that foundation today, which is Christ Jesus our Lord, to come to Him and say, "Lord,

> Nothing in my hand I bring,
> Simply to Thy cross I cling;
> Naked, come to Thee for dress;
> Helpless, look to Thee for grace;
> Foul, I to the fountain fly;
> Wash me, Saviour, or I die!"
>
> —Augustus M. Toplady

5. Overcoming the Foe

But it came to pass, that when Sanballat heard that we builded the wall, he was wroth, and took great indignation, and mocked the Jews.

And he spake before his brethren and the army of Samaria, and said, What do these feeble Jews? will they fortify themselves? will they sacrifice? will they make an end in a day? will they revive the stone out of the heaps of the rubbish which are burned?

Now Tobiah the Ammonite was by him, and he said, Even that which they build, if a fox go up, he shall even break down their stone wall.

Hear, O our God; for we are despised: and turn their reproach upon their own head, and give them for a prey in the land of captivity:

And cover not their iniquity, and let not their sin be blotted out from before thee: for they have provoked thee to anger before the builders.

So built we the wall; and all the wall was joined together unto the half thereof: for the people had a mind to work.

But it came to pass, that when Sanballat, and Tobiah, and the Arabians, and the Ammonites, and the Ash-dodites, heard that the walls of Jerusalem were made up, and that the breaches began to be stopped, then they were very wroth,

And conspired all of them together to come and to fight against Jerusalem, and to hinder it.

Nevertheless we made our prayer unto our God, and set a watch against them day and night, because of them.

—Nehemiah 4:1-9

WE ARE STUDYING the lifework of one of the greatest characters of the whole Bible. Nehemiah's courage and determination in the face of the fiercest opposition, his complete faith in God, his great passion for the service of his Lord: all of these things point him out as a man in a million, a man whose life is worth emulating, whose character is worth our close scrutiny and examination, and whose example—by the grace of God and the power of the indwelling Christ, through whom alone we can do anything—is worth reproducing. Indeed, the service of the Lord Jesus Christ today desperately needs men of the caliber of Nehemiah.

The story of this fourth chapter is thrilling indeed. If any of you think the Bible is a dull book, you can never have read the Book of Nehemiah.

Let me remind you that in the last chapter we left everybody hard at work rebuilding the wall of Jerusalem. As long as the wall of that city lay in ruins, the name of their God was brought to shame, and it was the recognition of that fact which was the inspiration of all their service for God. And I reminded you that as long as the walls of the New Jerusalem which God in Christ calls upon us to build (for we are laborers together with Him in the extension of His Kingdom and to the glory of His name), lie in ruins, whether it be in our personal life or in our church life, His name is being dishonored still. Indeed, more so, for the blood of Jesus has been shed, and we have the help of the Holy Spirit who has been sent down into our hearts to build upon the foundation of Jesus Christ Himself and to reproduce His life within each one of us. We saw how easily the walls of prayer, the walls of protection, the walls of purity, and the walls of passionate devotion can lie in ruins at our very door and bring shame upon the name of the Lord.

We observed that the general principles of allocation of labor appear to have been that every man repaired beside his own house. He was given that bit of wall in which he would naturally be expected to be the most interested, and incidentally and even more important, the bit of wall where the quality of his work would be the more readily tested by those who knew him best. How sad it is, indeed, that the place where the true quality of our Christian life is really tested, at home, is the place that it is so often sadly neglected. If we serve the church or serve the Lord at the expense of our duty to our loved ones and the responsibilities of our homes, there is something wrong with the balance of our Christian lives.

Here in chapter four we see the walls proceeding to go up, the opposition gathering its forces, and finally we read the thrilling story of the enemy's complete overthrow.

Let us examine the real nature of this opposition. As we do so, we are not looking into Old Testament history alone. I always find the Old Testament fascinating to preach from, for it is always an illustration of New Testament truth and twentieth century experience. As we see the tactics of the enemy in Nehemiah's day, we shall discover that he uses exactly the same tactics with us, and he used them against our Lord Jesus Christ also. We must examine the secret of overthrowing and defeating him, which was not only Nehemiah's but was also our Lord's, and must be ours if we would overcome.

Wherever a work is attempted for God, opposition is always first from without and then from within. It comes from external circumstances and from internal enemies. Here the first sign of opposition is from without and it takes the form of derision and scorn. "And he [Sanballat] spake before his brethren and the army of Samaria, and said, What do these feeble Jews? will they fortify themselves? will they sacrifice? will they make an end in a day? will they revive the stones out of the heaps of the rubbish which are burned? Now Tobiah the Ammonite was by him, and he said, Even that which they build, if a fox go up, he shall even break down their stone wall" (4:2, 3). Pretty crushing, isn't it? "Your personnel is completely weak. Your task it absolutely impossible. Even if you do start out, God isn't going to take any notice of you and He won't help you."

How subtle, how modern this approach! When the Christian dares to say that the only hope of the world is in the gospel of God's redeeming grace, the whole force of modern civilization and education lines up against him and says, "You, with your feeble prayer meetings. You, with your silly little plan of getting people converted one by one. How can that possibly stand alongside our great socializing economic program in which a whole world can be revolutionized in a few years? You feeble little lot!"

The world judges everything by size, by headlines, by

imposing schemes, by vast advertisements, and it pours contempt upon the feeble little flock of the people of God. "You have no intellect. You are out of date. You have no money. You have no status." How the world talks about you! But the tragedy is that too often the thinking of the world has infiltrated the church so that even Christian people seem to believe that to accomplish anything for God you must prove to the world that you can put on something big. I have every regard for mass evangelism, and I appreciate its value in a city, but New Testament methods never put on a splash and they don't depend upon machinery and famous personalities and publicity. God's work depends on everyone with a mind to work who will be on the job seven days a week, night and day.

When we say that religious revival is the greatest need of our time, the scornful reply is, "You really believe that something you call revival can bring to pass that which all the world's best brains have failed to accomplish?" Or when we say that one urgent need is for prayer, the sarcastic answer is, "Fancy thinking that the God of all the universe is going to take any notice of you! If God has any interest in the affairs of the world, why doesn't He do something to get it out of the mess it is in, without prayer meetings?" Yes, whenever a work of God is begun, in heart or home, Satan uses the method of scorn. The sad thing is that Satan often employs professing Christian people to give utterance to these discouraging thoughts. Sometimes it comes from those who are very close to us, and sometimes it hurts desperately.

There is the scorn of the husband heaped upon the wife who receives Christ and is going to seek to live for Him;

the scorn of the father and mother whose children express a desire to equip themselves for Christian service; the scorn of the sweetheart when her lover dares to suggest that their love for each other must be centered in the Lord, and that He must come first. The scorn of the self-righteous for the man who listens to the message of the Spirit-filled life: "That's fanatical, that's extreme! You have all that you need in Jesus from the moment of your conversion. Don't expect anything more"—Satan is seeking to quench the desire for a deeper Christian life by making a man believe that because his position in heaven is eternally secure nothing else matters. If you think this is strange doctrine, examine your New Testament. I tell you, I never live one day of my life without my heart being hungry for more and more of Jesus. But the scorn and the sarcasm of the world hurts deeply when it is expressed on the lips of those who love us and whom we love.

The opposition was not only scornful but it was very powerful. Look at it: Sanballat, Tobiah, the Arabians, the Ammonites, the Ashdodites. What a formidable alliance! How amazing that warring factions have suddenly sunk all their differences and have come together to crush Nehemiah! Mutual enemies have become mutual friends in their determined effort to stamp out a work for God.

This kind of thing hit the Lord Jesus Christ, too—that brings immense comfort to my heart. "And the men that held Jesus mocked him, and smote him" (Luke 22:63). "... And the rulers also ... derided him, saying, He saved others; let him save himself, if he be Christ, the chosen of God. And the soldiers also mocked him ... saying, If thou be king of the Jews, save thyself" (Luke 23:35-37)

—scorn, shame, sarcasm, and withering, biting opposition. "And the same day Pilate and Herod were made friends together: for before they were at enmity between themselves" (Luke 23:12). Whatever scorn has ever been directed against you has first of all been poured out upon our precious Lord. And, my fellow believer, the disciple is never above his Master.

If some of you are thinking to yourself, "What is he talking about? I have no scorn heaped upon me. I suppose that some queer Christian people have a great deal of ridicule because they are really peculiar or extreme"—take care, do not sit there and congratulate yourself. Perhaps it is because Satan doesn't think you are worth bothering about.

Notice how hard those people worked at that wall—almost as if they were going to finish it in one day. It took them fifty-two, which was quick work at that, but they labored at it so desperately that it looked as if they were trying to do it in a day. It was that spirit which roused the attack of the enemy. He never bothers about half-hearted Christian people, but once you are desperate for God and become burdened for the salvation of men, then all hell will oppose you.

Sanballat's scorn was only a cloak for something else, however. What was it? Verse 1: "Sanballat . . . was wroth. . . ." The scorn and derision of the enemy simply hid his anger. What was he angry about? The fact was that he had no logical reason to keep Nehemiah from building up those walls. He had no sound argument against it, and therefore he was desperately angry that someone should come along and do this thing. And if people jeer at our Christian testimony today, it is because they have no argument against the gospel. The world will always be angry at any message which exposes sin. If a preacher dares to emphasize the truth that the New Testament demands repentance, that behind all saving faith there must be a deliberate turning from sin before there can be any blessing, that the gospel ruthlessly exposes our tragic condition and our utter bankruptcy before it applies the balm of Gilead —I'm telling you, the world will always be angry at a message like that.

Now, how was the opposition overcome? Did Nehemiah panic or get very worried? Did he answer back or retaliate? Not a bit of it. What did he do? Verse 6: "So built we the wall. . . ." I think that is a magnificent statement. He just kept on building and ignored them, for "the people had a mind to work." God's people did not mope over the difficulties, nor did they find fault or chatter or gossip; neither did they answer back or retaliate; they simply concentrated on doing the thing that God had called them to do.

My friend, that's how the Lord Jesus overcame for us. ". . . when he was reviled, [he] reviled not again . . . but committed himself to him that judgeth righteously" (I Peter 2:23). ". . . he is brought as a lamb to the slaughter, and as a sheep before her shearers is dumb, so he openeth not his mouth" (Isaiah 53:7). He just went right through until, at the end of it all, having come through all that hell could concentrate upon Him, He cried, as He hung upon a tree, "It is finished!" So heaven was opened from that day to every guilty sinner who comes to God through faith in the atoning blood of Jesus. *That* is how He overcame.

When the scorn, sarcasm and opposition of the enemy

are flooding in upon your life, no matter if it be from your nearest and dearest associate and colleague, your friend or loved one, you may ask, "How am *I* to overcome? By answering scorn with scorn?" No, answering back is out of the Christian's vocabulary altogether. ". . . I laboured," said the Apostle, "more abundantly than they all: yet not I, but the grace of God which was with me" (I Corinthians 15:10). A *mind* to work? Of course, let me say this in passing so that you get the clear picture: they didn't *all* have a mind to work. A glance back at the third chapter, the fifth verse, would tell you that there were a few noblemen who refused to bend their necks to the job. We know that sort of people, don't we? They send their donations and we give them a receipt for income tax purposes. We do not despise the giving of all who wish to contribute to the Lord's work, but if there be some people who imagine that by doing that kind of thing they are discharging their missionary responsibility, well, my friend, you need to challenge your own heart.

"The people had a *mind* to work," said Nehemiah, and in the New Testament the Apostle Paul exhorts us: "Let this *mind* be in you, which was also in Christ Jesus: Who . . . thought it not robbery to be equal with God, But . . . humbled himself, and became obedient unto death, even the death of the cross" (Philippians 2:5-8). ". . . I am among you," the Lord Jesus said, "as he that serveth" (Luke 22:27). ". . . the son of man came not to be ministered unto, but to minister . . ." (Mark 10:45). How am I to answer Him? O Lord Jesus, give me Thy mind, Thy mind to serve, Thy mind to work, Thy mind to labor, Thy mind to strive.

> I cannot work my soul to save,
> For that my Lord hath done;
> But I will work like any slave,
> For love of God's dear Son.

The people not only had a mind to work, they also had a heart to pray. "... we made our prayer unto our God ..." (4:9). In the Christian life, if we have no heart to pray, we have no mind to work. Have you noticed if you forget to pray, or feel you have no time to pray, how irritable and critical you get? If you have no heart to pray, do not go on working. Jesus overcame with whole nights of prayer, with sweat and blood in the garden of Gethsemane, as He triumphed in doing the will of God.

Have you learned to pray as the disciples prayed in the early church when the opposition was fierce and intense? Listen to them: "Lord, behold their threatenings: and grant unto thy servants, that with all boldness they may speak thy word ... and that signs and wonders may be done by the name of thy holy child Jesus" (Acts 4:29, 30). We do not care about the sarcasm of others, if only we can produce demonstrations today that the risen Lord Jesus still transforms surrendered hearts and lives.

A mind to work, a heart to pray, and an eye to watch: "... we ... set a watch against them day and night ..." (4:9). The thing that appeals to me about Nehemiah more than anything is that he was such a practical fellow. He was not one of those people of whom it is sometimes said that they are too heavenly minded to be any earthly use. He kept his feet on the ground. He knew how to organize, and he knew how to agonize. Now this man determined that as he prayed and worked, he would also see to it that there

was a sentry on duty night and day, and that every section
of that wall should be guarded by the sleepless vigil of a
man who watched for the unexpected attack of the enemy.

We can say, "Lord Jesus, wilt Thou be the Sentry outside *my* life, night and day?" "The peace of God," said the
Apostle Paul, "shall garrison [shall stand guard, shall stand
as a sentry] over your hearts and minds through Christ
Jesus" (Philippians 4:7).

How lovely it is, when the day's battles are over, to lie
down on the Saviour's breast and say to Him as you lapse
into unconsciousness, "Lord Jesus, I'm going to sleep now,
but You never slumber nor sleep. Watch over me tonight.
Watch over my unconscious thinking; may my dreams be
of Thee. Watch over my waking moments, and when I
awake, may my first thought be of Thyself." There lies the
victory: all in our precious Lord who has been "in all points
tempted like as we are, yet without sin" (Hebrews 4:15).

Let me say as I close this chapter that it is one of Satan's
greatest victories when he just laughs you out of a work
for God. Unfortunately, he manages it far too often, simply
by his scorn and sarcasm and derision; somehow the wall
remains broken down. How I pray that we may have learned
our lesson from Nehemiah, but more than that, from our
Saviour Himself, and that we will be less concerned about
the ridicule of men and much more concerned about the
approval of our God. "So built we the wall."

I want to ask you one question that I cannot give the
answer to, but which *you* must answer if the Lord is really
speaking to your heart: in the building of a work for God,
are you serving Him, or are you opposing? Are you on the
Lord's side, or are you on Sanballat's side? If you're on the

wrong side, may God give you grace today to change sides and get onto the side of triumph and victory, and have a mind to work and a heart to pray and an eye to watch. So, by God's goodness, we shall build the wall.

6. Removing Rubbish

And Judah said, The strength of the bearers of burdens is decayed, and there is much rubbish; so that we are not able to build the wall.

—Nehemiah 4:10

NEHEMIAH 4:10 is an Old Testament illustration of New Testament truth: "And Judah said, The strength of the bearers of burdens is decayed, and there is much rubbish; so that we are not able to build the wall." Paul said, "We are troubled on every side, yet not distressed; we are perplexed, but not in despair; Persecuted, but not forsaken; cast down, but not destroyed" (II Corinthians 4:8, 9).

It is a source of great comfort to me, and I am sure to every Christian, to turn to the Bible and to discover that all through history men of God who ventured upon a service for God have been confronted with the very same problems that constantly vex us. Here is Nehemiah, unmistakably called of God, commissioned by the king, having secured an army of helpers to work upon rebuilding the wall, who now finds himself faced with discouragement of every possible kind.

At first it seemed that everything was going wonderfully. The king was very glad to equip him for his journey and send him to Jerusalem. There he prayerfully surveyed the ruins, and he soon had around him a great army of people who were ready to shoulder the burden of rebuilding. But so often, immediately following a time of blessing, the enemy counterattacks. The opposition of Sanballat, Tobiah and Gesham, who had already launched their campaign of hate, had been faced realistically. We saw that <u>God's people</u> <u>had a mind to work</u>, <u>a heart to pray</u>, and <u>an eye to watch</u>, and therefore, for the time being at least, these enemies were held at bay.

But here we find something even more serious, for <u>in every Christian</u> advance with God we find that two kinds of <u>foes arise</u>—<u>one external</u> and <u>the other internal</u>. Here is internal trouble striking at Nehemiah. Judah said, "There is decaying strength, accumulating rubbish, and an impossible task." A wonderful comfort to Nehemiah it must have been to hear that!

You notice who said it, don't you? Judah, of all people! Of him long ago it had been said that his foot should be on the neck of his enemies. "The sceptre shall not depart from Judah, nor a lawgiver from between his feet, until Shiloh come . . ." (Genesis 49:10). Here is the cream of the army, the crack regiment, threatening to revolt, filled with discouragement. "We're getting weak and feeble, with too much rubbish and too big a job to face." Of course Nehemiah had expected trouble from Sanballat and all the rest of them, and no doubt from some of his nominal adherents who set out to build because everybody else did, but Judah—what a sickening sense of being let down must have overwhelmed Nehemiah when Judah came to him with that statement!

How easy it would have been simply to give in, to go back to Persia and be a cupbearer again; but I find no indication that Nehemiah even contemplated it. <u>A man called of God is sure of himself in the sense that he is sure of God's enablings</u>, and <u>even though he may have to stand absolutely alone</u>, <u>retreat is never in his vocabulary</u>.

What a powerful weapon is this which the enemy thrusts into our souls—when the cream of the army threatens desertion, when the prayer partners become discouraged, when the fellow missionary threatens to return home because it is too tough at this station, when those who should be sharing the burden most deeply with the Nehemiahs of our time have no vision at all. How disheartening it is when those who should be right in the thick of the fight in real prayer warfare are men and women without any vision, without any burden! They will do the same job and carry on the same work as they have done it for years, but they do not seem to be capable of real heart travail. Those who should be prayer partners think the task is too much to handle, "We just can't do it!"

Of course, the burdens which had to be carried in Nehemiah's day were very great indeed; I don't underestimate them. Nebuchadnezzer had made a thorough job of destroying Jerusalem; he had not left one stone on top of another. It was absolutely hopeless to start rebuilding until the excavation work had been completed, and until the original foundations had all been exposed. To risk putting up those walls on the rubbish would simply have meant that before they were completed they would have fallen down again. It was essential that the foundation should be cleared away and the work should be built upon the rock.

To any but a man of discernment, of course, that was not only extremely tiresome and unspectacular, but it was also a dangerous waste of time. These walls had been down long enough; the city had been exposed to attack far too long. But if these walls were to stand, they had to be built on solid foundations, and therefore every bit of rubbish had to be cleared away until the foundations were exposed. Before the walls could be built, there was a great deal of underground work to be done. Before they started building the walls upward, they had to have the foundations downward. Before they could bear fruit outwardly, they had to bear fruit inwardly. They had to go down before they could go up.

Now, my friends, let me remind you that the church has had to contend with rubbish all through its history: the paganism and superstition of the vast Roman Empire, the mythology of Greece, false philosophies, traditions, prejudices, and spurious religions have littered her path all through time. All these, and more, have constantly sought to keep back the building of the walls. But through all the years, God has matched the rubbish-makers with excavators, and all through church history God has produced His men who would deal with the rubbish ruthlessly and fearlessly. From the time of Paul to the days of the Reformation we hear that triumphant cry, "Let's clear everything out of the way and get through to God!" Martin Luther cleared away rubbish and rediscovered the great foundation doctrine of justification by faith. He was followed by Calvin with his reminder of the great covenant of sovereign grace, by Zwingli, and by John Knox, who cried, "O God, give me Scotland or I die!" Wesley, Whitfield, D. L. Moody, and hundreds more have emerged in recent generations to deal with the excavating work, to lay bare the foundation upon which no other man can build, for "Except the Lord build the house, they labour in vain that build it . . ." (Psalm 127:1).

In every section of the church of Christ the battle rages

yet. Of course, in any work for God there always have been, and always will be, some people who will defend the existence of any heap of rubbish, no matter how unsavory or how useless it may be. There are some folks who will always find an excuse why that bit of rubbish should not be disturbed: "After all, they founded the organization . . . it's been in existence since we began. It mustn't be disturbed; leave it alone, at any cost." And it's sheer rubbish! Long since it has ceased to be an evangelizing factor in the work of God.

I have no doubt there are some who might advocate a rapid building up of church work which, at least, can be seen by other people. "Let's put on a great program! Let's call in a great personality! Let's have a massive campaign! Let's advertise—put placards all over the city. Let's do something that is going to appeal to the crowds. But this work or that work, this organization or that organization has been here a long time—don't touch that." No doubt in many churches today there would be those who advocate introducing more social life, introducing motion pictures, introducing this and that—doing something to attract the people.

Deliberately we turn our backs upon all that line of argument. Let me say to you with deep conviction that the work of excavating must come first; the rubbish must go, and every part of the life of any church which is not directly evangelizing, and which is not now a real soul-winning factor, cannot justify its existence by mere history. The foundation must be laid bare, the foundation which is Jesus Christ our Lord, and upon that basis the church must build gold and silver and precious stones, and clear

away the wood, hay and stubble (I Corinthians 3:12).
Everything else must go, no matter how painful it might
be.

The Lord is speaking, however, not only about rubbish
in the church, but rubbish in the hearts of Christian people.
". . . know ye not that your body is the temple of the Holy
Ghost?" (I Corinthians 6:19). There is a building going up
today in each one of us, and there is much rubbish. "If any
man," said Paul, "defile the temple of God, him shall God
destroy; for the temple of God is holy, which temple ye
are" (I Corinthians 3:17). Have you ever stopped to think
how much the blood of Jesus Christ was shed to accomplish
in your life, how much the power of the indwelling Spirit
of God is there to do, but how little, in fact, has been done?

I confess to you that almost every day a fresh heap of
rubbish is discovered in my life which I hardly knew existed.
Points in which we thought we were strong—when we are
honest with ourselves in the presence of God—we discover
are the very points in which we are weak. There was, perhaps, some sin from which we had thought we were set
free in our childhood and because of that we were particularly severe with other people when they were trapped
by it. Alas, we have discovered that it has broken out in
our hearts.

All the rubbish: pride, unbelief, anger and temper, des-
pondence, self-importance, evil desire—the rubbish of a
careless, dry, barren life—what a foul heap it all is, and
the building of the temple of the Holy Spirit has been
retarded because of it.

More subtle still, perhaps, is that many of us, through
wonderful seasons of prayer and great conferences, have at

last thought that we have attained to a degree of spirituality
where old failures are behind us forever. Some time before
I left Britain, I was preaching in a church in Southhampton,
and afterwards a young fellow with his face aglow came
up to me, and he almost threw his arms around my neck.
He said, "Hallelujah, brother," and I took a deep breath and
said, "Hallelujah," and hoped it was all right. I didn't quite
know what he was going to say next.

He said, "I want you to know that eighteen months ago
I was saved, twelve months ago I was sanctified, and now
I am completely free from sin."

I looked at him and replied, "My dear friend, you've
got further in eighteen months than I've got in twenty-
five years. And if I read my New Testament aright, you've
got further in eighteen months than the Apostle Paul got
in a lifetime." For at the end of Paul's story (somehow I
feel it's going to be the end of the story with me and with
many others), he declared, "Lord, I'm the chief of sinners."

There is no place where I can stay secure except at the
foot of the cross. Let no man deceive himself; "If we say
that we have no sin," said the Apostle John, "we deceive
ourselves, and the truth is not in us" (I John 1:8). If any
man imagines that he has got some experience of the Holy
Spirit and some experience of Christ which has put past
sins behind him forever, let him get the garbage truck out
and fill it up with such rubbish. Learn today, with the Apostle Paul, that ". . . in me (that is, in my flesh,) dwelleth no
good thing . . ." (Romans 7:18). Down at Calvary is the
only place for us all, for in Jesus Christ alone is all our
glorying; He is made unto us wisdom and righteousness
and sanctification and redemption. If we are anything it is

only by the grace of God, and the power of His blood, and
the control of the Spirit.

What then can we do about this rubbish that exists in
churches, and also in our hearts? Is there nothing we can
do about it? Do we simply sit back and do nothing, and let
God do it all?

Most certainly not, and I want to give you three pre-
scriptions for filling the garbage truck. The first is: be sure
that the foundation of your life is firmly laid. Make sure
that it is clearly exposed, and that by faith you stand on
that foundation which no man can lay, which is Jesus Christ
our Lord. Are you sure of that? Or are you simply building
your life on the sand?

It is wonderful to watch a little child take a bucket and
spade to the seaside and fill that bucket with sand, turn it
over and build sand piles. Then watch the tide come in,
and see the child's eyes when the sand has disappeared and
the castle has gone: "Daddy, where has it gone to?" I have
never been able to answer that question satisfactorily. All
that has happened is that the ocean has come in and swept it
away.

In your life and mine there is a river which all of us are
going to cross, and one day you are going to stand at the
brink and pass through; your body is going to be left behind, and your soul is going on to hell or heaven. Are you
building on the Rock? Are you on the solid ground which
is Christ our Lord, or is it only sinking, shifting sand? Be
sure you are on the foundation.

In the second place, remember that you are the temple
of the Holy Spirit; it is His work to build it. He began it,
you know. He digged down until He exposed our empti-

ness, until He cast out our self-righteousness and laid the foundation of Christ Himself within us where the shifting sand of self had been—that is conversion. Has that happened to you? It is not just holding up your hand or coming forward or signing a card, but it is the Holy Spirit digging deep and exposing self, and in that corrupt ruin where self had been, Jesus Christ has become established. He did all that and He has done everything else which ever will stand the test of time and eternity. Anything we attempt in our own strength toward building that temple is in vain. Holiness, certainly, is to be sought with all our hearts, but it can only be attained by faith in Jesus.

In that precious chapter of God's Word, Ephesians 5, Paul says that it is the bridegroom, not the bride, who is to make the bride fit to meet her husband. ". . . Christ also loved the church, and gave himself for it; That he might sanctify and cleanse it with the washing of water by the word, That he might present it to himself a glorious church, not having spot, or wrinkle, or any such thing; but that it should be holy and without blemish" (5:25-27). The building of the temple of the Spirit within you is His work.

But then, in the third place, we are to build, also, for we are laborers together with God. We are to build this temple with all *His* power and all *His* strength and all *His* enabling. How are we to build? In II Peter 1:5-7 we read that we are to add to our faith virtue, and then on top of virtue, knowledge, and on top of knowledge, self-control, and on top of self-control, patience, and on top of patience, godliness, and over godliness, brotherly kindness, and then the crowning stone that makes it all so lovely, on top of all, love.

"We are building day by day, at our work and in our

play," sing the children. Are you building that kind of material into the temple of His Spirit? Have you a faith which rests solidly in the blood, and upon that faith is there being built gold and silver and precious stones, the fruit of the indwelling Christ? For Peter goes on to say, "For if these things be in you, and abound, they make you that ye shall neither be barren nor unfruitful in the knowledge of our Lord Jesus Christ" (v. 8).

Whatever sin there may be within us, the Holy Spirit is there to conquer it, and the blood of Christ answers for us in heaven and cleanses us from it in the sight of God. Confess it to Him and know that you are forgiven. Conquer it in the power of the Spirit within you and He will perfect that which is within each one of us. And as we labor together in the church and labor together in our lives, as we seek to build upon a solid foundation, let us never be satisfied until that day when we shall awake in His likeness.

A very favorite verse of mine says,

> May the mind of Christ my Saviour
>   Live in me from day to day,
> By His love and power controlling
>   All I do and say.

> May the Word of God dwell richly
>   In my heart from hour to hour,
> So that all may see I triumph
>   Only through His power.

* * *

> May the love of Jesus fill me,
>   As the waters fill the sea;
> Him exalting, self abasing,
>   This is victory.

May I run the race before me,
Strong and brave to face the foe,
Looking only unto Jesus
As I onward go.

May His beauty rest upon me
As I seek the lost to win,
And may they forget the channel,
Seeing only Him.

"The strength of the burden-bearers is decayed. There is much rubbish; we cannot build the wall," Judah complained. "But they that wait upon the Lord shall renew their strength . . ." (Isaiah 40:31). The indwelling Christ is ready at the door of your heart to fill the garbage truck with all the rubbish that you are willing to get rid of, and by the grace of God and by the power of His Spirit, we will build the wall upon the foundation that will stand firm for time and eternity.

7. Building and Battling

And our adversaries said, They shall not know, neither see, till we come in the midst among them, and slay them, and cause the work to cease.

And it came to pass, that when the Jews which dwelt by them came, they said unto us ten times, From all places whence ye shall return unto us they will be upon you.

Therefore set I in the lower places behind the wall, and on the higher places, I even set the people after their families with their swords, their spears, and their bows.

And I looked, and rose up, and said unto the nobles, and to the rulers, and to the rest of the people, Be not ye afraid of them: remember the Lord, which is great and terrible, and fight for your brethren, your sons, and your daughters, your wives, and your houses.

And it came to pass, when our enemies heard that it was known unto us, and God had brought their counsel to nought, that we returned all of us to the wall, every one unto his work.

And it came to pass from that time forth, that the half of my servants wrought in the work, and the other half of them held both the spears, the shields, and the bows, and the habergeons; and the rulers were behind all the house of Judah.

They which builded on the wall, and they that bare burdens, with those that laded, every one with one of his hands wrought in the work, and with the other hand held a weapon.

For the builders, every one had his sword girded by his side, and so builded. And he that sounded the trumpet was by me.

And I said unto the nobles, and to the rulers, and to the rest of the people, The work is great and large, and we are separated upon the wall, one far from another.

In what place therefore ye hear the sound of the trumpet, resort ye thither unto us: our God shall fight for us.

So we laboured in the work: and half of them held the spears from the rising of the morning till the stars appeared.

Likewise at the same time said I unto the people, Let every one with his servant lodge within Jerusalem, that in the night they may be a guard to us, and labour on the day.

So neither I, nor my brethren, nor my servants, nor the men of the guard which followed me, none of us put off our clothes, saving that every one put them off for washing.

—Nehemiah 4:11-23

As we have been studying this very wonderful Book of Nehemiah, perhaps it is well to recall the progress that has been made in the task to which this man was called, the rebuilding of the wall of Jerusalem. We are told in the sixth verse of chapter four that "all the wall was joined together unto the half thereof." In other words, they have reached the halfway stage. The task was half finished, and I suggest to you that in any work for God, or in any Christian experience, that is the hardest place of all.

I wonder if you have ever tried to do a bit of mountaineering? Maybe you have stood at the foot of a mountain and seen far away there in the clear blue sky what you imagined was the peak, and you set out to climb. You found it very thrilling as you started out, but as you went up that mountainside you found it getting steeper and steeper, and rockier and rockier, and your progress was slower and slower, your breath louder and louder. Presently you stopped and looked back to see the progress that you had made. Then you looked up to the peak, and you discovered that you were only about halfway there. Actually, what you had thought from ground level was the top of the mountain was merely a promontory, and there was much more of that mountain out of sight which you had only now discovered. As you see how far you have yet to go and take stock of your present condition of breathlessness and exhaustion, you say to yourself, "This is quite beyond me. I'd better go down again."

The halfway stage is the toughest of all. When the initial enthusiasm for some project has departed, when the funds have been raised or the building has been put up, or whatever it may be, when the organization has started off, the initial push has somehow departed and you are more and more conscious, not so much of what has already been done, but of what is yet to be done: you are increasingly impressed with the magnitude of the unfinished task. Just then is the toughest bit of all.

Now that is also true in the Christian life, when the early days of conversion are past and the early experiences of the wonder of God's salvation. Perhaps the vigor of young manhood and young womanhood has departed from you, and yet in the normal course of events life's journey is still a long road to travel. You are beginning to find that the Christian battle has taken out of you more than you had imagined, and it has cost you far more than you ever dreamed—nobody had ever told you what it would really mean to be a Christian and to live for God. Maybe in the very heat of the battle, with the fight raging around you, you are beginning to ask yourself, "How shall I ever get through to the end of the journey?"

I want to speak to people who feel like that: people who are in the thick of the fight, right in the front line, on the firing line for God, people who know something of the conflict of Christian living and who are finding the battle hard going and are thinking to themselves, "It's such a long journey yet! Shall I ever make it?"

We will notice four things in this chapter which I trust

may bring comfort and blessing. First of all—perhaps not much of a comfort but something we all need to realize—there was an immediate renewal of the onslaught of the enemy. This was the appropriate moment for the enemy to launch his heaviest attack. At the moment when the wall was half up, when the task was only half completed and the people were getting weary of building the wall as well as of the burdens they had to carry: this was the psychological moment for a fresh onslaught from the enemy.

Notice that it took a twofold shape: it was first of all a campaign of talk—sheer, ruthless talk. But sarcasm, taunts and jeers having failed, now they are replaced by threats. Observe the ruthlessness of this attack. It was concerted: verse 8 tells us that they conspired, all of them together, to come and fight against Jerusalem—Sanballat, Tobiah, the Arabians, the Ammonites, the Ashdodites, forgetting their own private differences and their conflict between themselves, united together now to launch a full-scale frontal attack upon Nehemiah.

Verse 11 tells us, "They shall not know, neither see, till we come in the midst among them. . . ." This enemy was not at a distance here; he was closing in for a hand-to-hand conflict, to an immediate close pressure upon this work of God. It was cruel, for verse 11 tells us, "we will slay them." Now they were going to stop at nothing; they cared not about shedding blood. At any cost, the wall must not go up. It was confident, for they said, ". . . we . . . [shall] cause the work to cease."

Now we must recognize that there is a stage of Christian experience when the wall is half up, and you know what that means in terms of your own life. You are building for

God, and your body is the temple of the Holy Spirit. The work is half completed, as it were, much of life's journey lying yet before you. In relation to the work of the church, we are much more impressed with what has yet to be accomplished. And that is the moment when Satan comes to close grips with the child of God. Do you know anything about that experience?

Do you know anything about such a combat in prayer that is utterly, completely exhausting? Do you know what it means to feel that you can scarcely get through to God for the sheer pressure of the power of the enemy? What form does that take? Crowding upon our imagination come unholy thoughts, sensual desires, wrong actions. Pressing upon us are the drudgeries of daily life and the demands of business. Behind all such deadly antagonism to a work of God is Satan himself, using all the force at his command to keep back the building up of the temple of the Holy Spirit.

Of course, because their enemies were so strong, the reaction in the camp of Nehemiah was fear, for verse 12 tells us, ". . . when the Jews which dwelt by them came, they said unto us ten times, From all places whence ye shall return unto us they will be upon you." Some of Nehemiah's people, who apparently had no zeal for the work of God and were all too eager to spread alarmist reports, brought news of a second attack. I have studied pretty closely the translation of verse 12. It is a little vague; in the Hebrew, as a matter of fact, it scarcely makes sense. It may be that they were so out of breath that they were incoherent when they brought in their report, but I think we would not be so far off if we read it this way: "Whatever place you turn to they are against us, so you need to be on your guard on all sides."

Here were the pessimists. "Nehemiah," they said, "wherever you go they are all against you. Whatever direction you turn, they are there. You will have to have eyes at the back of your head and be on guard on every side. Nehemiah, you're hemmed in and surrounded and the situation is really hopeless." Of course, that report spread fear among Nehemiah's soldiers, and we are told in verse 14 of this chapter that even the nobles and the rulers were affected. Once again in our story Nehemiah appears to stand alone, and yet not alone, for even then he could pray as did the Apostle Paul later, ". . . all men forsook me . . . Notwithstanding the Lord stood with me, and strengthened me . . ." (II Timothy 4:16, 17).

Force and fear: ruthless, relentless pressure of satanic power was bringing fear to the people of God. Should sheer satanic pressure bring fear into the church? Never! Why did it here? I can tell you why. There were some people there who lived near the enemy. That is the clue, for they were not in touch with the glow of spiritual force and power. They were not living sufficiently near the center of things to share the thrill and the joy of the battle and the victory, and to see God at work. All they were conscious of was the opposition.

I wonder how many Christian people are living dangerously near the enemy. They have no close contact with God's work, no intimate fellowship with Jesus Christ, no real heart communion with their God. They are very near the enemy. And the symptoms of that are these: you begin to think upon a work of God and you say to yourself, "It's too big. The days are too tough and the circumstances are too hard, and the pressure of evil is too strong. I don't think we will ever make it." And so you begin to spread discouragement in the ranks of God's people.

Nobody ever comes to a church service and has a neutral effect upon it. No one simply sits down as a kind of spectator to a program, because if we could only see with spiritual insight into the true character of services in the house of God, we would see that we are conducting a spiritual warfare—on the one hand seeking to press home the claims of Christ, on the other hand seeking to defeat the powers of darkness—and everybody affects the spiritual temperature of the whole. The person who lives in league with the enemy, who has no zeal for the work of God, who is only a kind of onlooker, that man ruins the spiritual temperature of the whole fellowship. He has lost the glow and the radiance and is out of touch with reality.

What tremendous pressure, therefore, this man Nehemiah had to contend with—an immense force which had resulted in fear of an attack!

In the second place, would you just pause a moment to recognize the reason for this opposition? We must examine the causes. Why all the fury? Why all the trouble? Has Nehemiah done them any wrong? Has he interfered with them? No, not at all. Verse 7 tells us the reason for their anger: ". . . when . . . [they] heard that the walls of Jerusalem were made up, and that the breaches began to be stopped, then they were very wroth." The only reason for the fury of the enemy was the demonstration of the power of God. It is always so.

Satan, the archenemy of Christ, has one focal point

of attack here on earth: the executive of the Godhead—
the Holy Spirit. And whenever our enemy sees a work of
the Spirit he concentrates all his forces against it. That was
true in the lifetime of our Lord Jesus. His character, His
life, anointed constantly by the power of the Holy Spirit,
was such a condemnation of the hypocrisy of other people
that it kindled in them a flame of hatred and bitterness. It
was true in the life of the first martyr of the Christian faith:
Stephen, full of faith and of the Holy Spirit, was stoned
to death by the enemy.

The very fact that a work is of God will always arouse
the opposition of the enemy. One life lived in the power
of the indwelling Christ will stir the hatred of men whose
sinful lives are challenged by way of contrast. I would ask
you to assess your own experience by that statement. Wherever the temple of the Holy Spirit is being built up in the
Christian heart and a work of grace is going on, if the child
of God is building upon the foundation which is Christ
and seeks to become more like the Lord, you can be sure
that such a life is arousing hatred, opposition and bitterness.
Is that true of your life or isn't it?

Satan is never an opponent of orthodoxy. It is well to
remember that. The Pharisees were the most orthodox
people you could find. Satan is never the opponent of
religion or of mere creed, but he is always antagonistic to
every evidence of Holy Spirit life. Through the Christian's
journey and through all his battle, Satan will do all in his
power to drag such a man down to prove that his strength
is greater than the strength of Jesus Himself. Does your
Christian life constitute a challenge? Does it arouse opposition? Or do you find yourself still tremendously popular

with worldly people? If you do, there is something wrong
with your testimony, for the Lord Jesus said: "Remember
the word that I said unto you, The servant is not greater
than his lord. If they have persecuted me, they will also
persecute you . . ." (John 15:20).

The reason for the opposition was simply that the wall
was going up, that the work of God was being accomplished, and that things were happening which aroused all
the antagonism of hell. The Christian church should never
be afraid of that. Indeed, my conviction is that we should
pray for more of it.

What was the reaction of Nehemiah in this situation? I
cannot escape the thrill of this fourteenth verse; it says,
and Nehemiah is giving his autobiography, "I looked . . ."
And at that moment, with all the pressure upon him, with
all the consciousness of fear in his own camp and doubt
and uncertainty among his people, aware of the ruthless
force of the enemy, what would he do? He just looked up!

Oh, dear child of God, in the heat of the battle and in
the thick of the fight, have you learned to do that? Maybe
you are not able to say very much or to utter a lengthy
prayer, but in your heart you look up. Jehoshaphat once
said, ". . . we have no might against this great company
that cometh against us; neither know we what to do: but
our eyes are upon thee" (II Chronicles 20:12). Are you
looking up, Christian? Nehemiah looked up. Taking all his
care and all his fears and all his griefs, he spread them before
God. That lightened the load.

My great fear for the Christian church today is this:
that it looks in every direction except upward. We look
to every contrivance, except to God. We seek in every

manner to deal with the situation, except looking up. We trust in our machinery, and in our organization; we look around for new ways of doing the job. But we don't look up! Perhaps that is why the prayer meetings in churches today are so small. Why is it that people will give any time and spare anything for work and organization, but how few will really spend time to wait upon God?

Suppose someone should come to you and suggest you attend one meeting or organization less a week, and make it a point to be regularly at the place of prayer? Would that not be evidence that the church is looking up?

In life and in Christian experience there are situations in which we can do absolutely nothing. It is perfectly right and safe then to trust in God, but beware lest faith becomes presumption. Today very often in some quarters there is an unintelligent zeal for God which is often in the name of ultra-spirituality, which simply puts an emotional presumption in place of taking reasonable precautions. If you try to secure yourself in the Christian life by prayer only, without watchfulness, you are boastful and you are tempting God. If we try without prayer by watchfulness only, we are proud, and in either case we forfeit God's protection. Have you learned that to pray without precaution is sheer presumption? Have you learned that to take precaution without prayer is a symptom of pride?

Observe therefore the following prayer of Nehemiah which issues a threefold battle cry. This man knew how to look up, but he also knew how to attack. How thrilling it is: in verse 14 he says, ". . . remember the Lord, which is great and terrible. . . ." "You are in His will, and you are doing His work; you are here because God has called—remember the Lord who is great and terrible."

We do not often think of God, in these modern days, as a great and terrible God, but He is, you know! He is far greater than all our enemies, and one day, when He comes to judge, to them He will seem very terrible. I believe that to recognize how great and terrible God is, is to realize how mean and despicable are our enemies. "For with God," says the Book, "nothing shall be impossible." Nehemiah said, "Remember, remember the Lord your God." "Look up to Him, and remember that you are in His will and doing His work." And then he asked them to reflect: ". . . fight for your brethren, your sons, and your daughters, your wives, and your houses." Everything was at stake in the battle; everything that was dear to them depended upon the outcome.

Is that not true of the Christian life today? We wage warfare for God as we seek to stand true to His Book, which is His Word, and to the great doctrines of our faith. It is also true that our homes and our children are at stake. In the midst of the secularism, materialism, and liberalism that sweep through this country and the world today, everything is in the balance. Remember the Lord your God; reflect upon the issues at stake.

And then, said Nehemiah, "Resist!" (v. 7). I want you to observe very carefully how he resisted. Half the people were put to building while the other half were holding weapons. Half were at work and half were at watch, changing duties to relieve fatigue, so it was said of them that they worked with a weapon in one hand and with a tool in the other. Here is a great principle: we must be armed for our warfare. Each of us can have the Sword of the Spirit, the Word of God. Yes, there is a place for battling, but I do want to emphasize that the battling of the Christian must never replace the building. The negative must never replace the positive. The wall has got to go up; the final answer of the Christian to the world is that the wall is being built, that the temple of the Holy Spirit is visible.

The final documentary evidence of the church is that a work is going on, that a wall is being built, that a life is being transformed. I believe that if Satan gets Christian people involved in controversy at the expense of capturing souls for Christ he has secured a master stroke. Men spend their lives in so-called "defense of truth," and defense of position, and neglect the main task of building. They fight over hairsplitting matters of doctrine while souls are perishing.

The enemy used force once against John Bunyan and flung him into the Bedford jail, but the wall went up because there he wrote *Pilgrim's Progress*. Five times they put Wesley in jail, but the wall went up and the Methodist revival spread like a plague. The enemy can use force and pressure, but the only answer is that the wall goes up. The best defense of truth and the best attack against error is to propogate the gospel, and to build up the Spirit-filled life. Nehemiah got on with the job even as he battled against the foe; his principle was never to leave the building for the battling.

To me the most thrilling thing in this whole passage is in verse 20, where we read that Nehemiah had a rallying point for his whole army. He kept a trumpeter always by his side, verse 18 tells us. You see, the work was large and the area was immense; the workers were widely scattered and they were all laboring together at the same time. Can you picture this great commander touring the walls, going around to all his workers and encouraging them, giving them instructions that at the sound of the trumpet they were to leave their work and rally around him for the final overthrow of the enemy? The focal point of all strategy was their commander, and at the sounding of that trumpet they were all to gather as one man to win the victory.

Need I comment? Oh, could we have a world-wide vision of the church today for a moment, could God open our eyes to see our missionaries scattered all over the world—the ranks are very thin, with many other lands cut off from fellowship and communication. The work is great and the area is immense, but wherever they be scattered, there is one mighty Commander-in-Chief, our Lord Jesus Christ.

He is the rallying point for us all, and one day the trumpet shall sound, the rallying call will come, and on that day we will be taken from our work to meet Him; one glorious day the enemy will be utterly overthrown. How thrilling it is to know today that we are in that fight! Although the struggle may be terrific, the onslaught tremendous, and the journey may seem to be long, we are all united together under our great Lord Jesus Christ. One day the journey will be over, the trumpet shall sound, and Jesus will come; one day our enemy will be finally vanquished.

8. Steering Clear of Trouble

And there was a great cry of the people *and* of their wives against their brethren the Jews.

For there were that said, We, our sons, and our daughters, are many: therefore we take up corn for them, that we may eat, and live.

Some also there were that said, We have mortgaged our lands, vineyards, and houses, that we might buy corn, because of the dearth.

There were also that said, We have borrowed money for the king's tribute, and that upon our lands and vineyards.

Yet now our flesh is as the flesh of our brethren, our children as their children: and, lo, we bring into bondage our sons and our daughters to be servants, and some of our daughters are brought unto bondage already: neither is it in our power to redeem them: for other men have our lands and vineyards.

And I was very angry when I heard their cry and these words.

Then I consulted with myself, and I rebuked the nobles, and the rulers, and said unto them, Ye exact usury, every one of his brother. And I set a great assembly against them.

And I said unto them, We after our ability have redeemed our brethren the Jews, which were sold unto the heathen; and will ye even sell your brethren? or shall they be sold unto us? Then held they their peace, and found nothing to answer.

Also I said, It is not good that ye do: ought ye not to walk in the fear of our God because of the reproach of the heathen our enemies?

I likewise, and my brethren, and my servants, might exact of them money and corn: I pray you, let us leave off this usury.

Restore, I pray you, to them, even this day, their lands, their vineyards, their oliveyards, and their houses, also the hundredth part of the money, and of the corn, the wine, and the oil, that ye exact of them.

Then said they, We will restore them, and will require nothing of them; so will we do as thou sayest. Then I called the priests, and took an oath of them, that they should do according to this promise.

Also I shook my lap, and said, So God shake out every man from his house, and from his labour, that performeth not this promise, even thus be he shaken out, and emptied. And all the congregation said, Amen, and praised the Lord. And the people did according to this promise.

Moreover from the time that I was appointed to be their governor in the land of Judah, from the twentieth year even unto the two and thirtieth year of Artaxerxes the king, that is, twelve years, I and my brethren have not eaten the bread of the governor.

But the former governors that had been before me were chargeable unto the people, and had taken of them bread and wine, beside forty shekels of silver; yea, even their servants bare rule over the people: but so did not I, because of the fear of God.

Yea, also I continued in the work of this wall, neither bought we any land: and all my servants were gathered thither unto the work.

Moreover there were at my table an hundred and fifty of the Jews and rulers, beside those that came unto us from among the heathen that are about us.

Now that which was prepared for me daily was one ox and six choice sheep; also fowls were prepared for me, and once in ten days store of all sorts of wine: yet for all this required not I the bread of the governor, because the bondage was heavy upon this people.

Think upon me, my God, for good, according to all that I have done for this people.

—Nehemiah 5:1-19

We come now to chapter five and find Nehemiah faced with further problems. The enemy of any work of God is a relentless foe who attacks first from this quarter and then from that and then from the other—never letting the children of God alone. But here we find Nehemiah resisting something that was not really an attack at all, and this was one of the most difficult problems he had to face in all his work, for this was the thing that nearly wrecked the whole project. It was internal dissention among his people; this had nothing to do with external enemies.

There was a food crisis in the Jerusalem area, a famine caused by the very large increase in population—the third verse tells about it. The country became overpopulated with the returning Jews and their large families. This was making immense demands upon the produce of the land, for there had probably been a neglect of tilling the land over the years of dispersion, and perhaps also neglect because of enthusiasm for rebuilding the wall.

Furthermore, heavy taxation was also bringing dissatisfaction. We see in verse 4 that the king who had sent Nehemiah on his way still had this country under his control, and the people were obliged to pay heavy taxes. All these factors added up to a serious food shortage.

Unfortunately, as always, there were people who were prepared to take advantage of the situation. It must have been very distressing to Nehemiah to find that they were his own people, the Jews. A few were rich, and because they were rich they immediately took the chance to "feather their nests" at other people's expense, to grant loans at high rates of interest; to make mortgages only under oppressive terms, to take into their homes the sons and daughters of other people as slaves and make it impossible for their parents ever to redeem them again. This whole unhealthy situation led to misunderstanding, trouble, and friction, doubt and suspicion among God's people. Those people who had been so united in objective became divided in affection, and Nehemiah found a situation developing that was threatening to bring to nothing the work of God.

One of the things that does most harm in God's work is dissention among His people. If you want a work of God ruined, just let misunderstanding, discouragement and mistrust arise. Though the people may be united in objective, they will be divided in their affection and the work cannot survive.

Let us try to discover how Nehemiah dealt with this situation. Here was a man in Christian leadership, if you like, in the leadership of a work of God, and here was a man who was faced with internal trouble in the work. How did he meet it?

". . . so did not I," said Nehemiah, "because of the fear of God" (v. 15). He was the governor of this country, as you will discover in the context of the chapter. The previous leaders had made it a practice to profit at the expense of the people. Regardless of the poverty or the slavery or the unjust conditions around him, the governor usually saw to it that he himself never suffered, and that his needs were cared for first. Therefore it would not have been at all surprising if Nehemiah had done the same thing. Here he was faced with a choice. It would not have surprised the people if he had indulged in the same practice. But he saw that such a self-indulgent standard of living was threatening the whole testimony of God. He might have accepted the premise, "Everybody's doing it," but Nehemiah said, ". . . so did not I." He took a stand about it.

Nehemiah did not deal with this situation on the basis of organization or of argument, but rather on the basis of a life that was absolutely beyond suspicion. And because he, in his place of leadership, was able to face the whole company of his people and say, ". . . so did not I," the devil was confounded and the building of the wall went on.

The church of Christ in any work which it is trying to build up for the glory of God is going to be attacked far more by internal dissention than by outward opposition, and the basis of trouble is usually a general acceptance of a wrong standard of life.

Let me show you what I mean: in this statement of Nehemiah, who was able to face the people and say, ". . . so did not I, because of the fear of God," I observe three essential principles which, if the church of Christ and the Christian would follow them, would make their life and service victorious.

First, there is an attitude that must be maintained. "So did not I." Unless you and I as Christian people can say that frequently to the vain practices of our day, our life and testimony will be a failure. That sort of refusal to comply with custom, to follow the crowd is, I believe, the foundation stone, the bedrock of Christian integrity of life. It is

so easy to do as other people do, partly because of coward-
ice, and partly because of an instinctive desire to be like
other people. It is easy to think that because thousands of
people live their Christian lives upon a certain level, we can
do the same. It saves such a lot of bother if, when you are in
Rome, you do as Rome does. I believe that this attitude in
Christian circles today can be fatal. Nehemiah challenges us
all in his autobiography: ". . . so did not I, because of the
fear of God."

We can apply this principle in the first instance to the
great truths of our Christian faith, to evangelical doctrines.
Many people are being talked out of believing in the Bible
because they listen to others. Some men say you cannot
believe this or that, and they hold the great foundation
truths of the Christian faith in disrepute. Many people are
being persuaded that they cannot be considered intelligent or
well educated if they insist on the doctrine of the verbal
inspiration of the Book. Let me say to you that truth has
always lived with the minority; what the majority says at a
given moment is usually wrong. The crowd one day cried,
"Crucify him," and the whole world united to murder the
Son of God, because in their ignorance they knew Him
not.

We need to be careful that we do not yield one jot or
tittle of our conviction concerning the Book from which
we preach. But we need to hold those truths in charity and
in love and in consideration for others who may believe dif-
ferently. But *this* is the sword of the Spirit and *this* is the
Word of God, and upon this Book was the church founded
and upon this Book alone can the church grow.

The principle we learn from Nehemiah in the second

place is to avoid worldliness. Who is to draw the line for the Christian as to what he should do and should not do, as to where he should go and should not go? Who can be another man's conscience as to how far he may go in the matter of worldliness? But Nehemiah, in a time of confusion and misunderstanding, was able to stand before his people with a life that was above reproach.

One time when I was preaching in the north of England, a young lady received Christ as her Saviour in an evangelistic meeting, and she came to speak to me after one of the services.

I said to her, "We have a young people's meeting here on Saturday. I hope you will come back."

"Oh," she said, "I'm sorry, but I can't. I have a date."

"That's interesting," I said. "Where is that?"

"Well," she admitted, "it's a dance."

"Oh," I replied, "that's all right. You go, but remember that you belong to the Lord Jesus. And you'll testify, won't you, and you'll speak of Him?"

"Oh yes," she said, "certainly."

On Sunday night she was in the front row of the congregation, looking a little bit uncertain of herself, I thought. When the service was over, I went to speak to her.

"Did you enjoy your evening?" I asked.

"Well," she said, "not exactly."

"Tell me," I said. "What happened?"

"You see, I was dancing last night with my partner when I suddenly remembered my promise," she said. "I thought, 'I've got to do something about this.' So I screwed up my courage and looked at this man with whom I was dancing and said, 'Excuse me, but are you a Christian?'

"He looked at me," she said, "and replied, 'Good heavens, no! Are you?' And I said, 'Y-y-yes, I am.' And do you know what he said to me? He just looked me straight in the face and said, 'What in God's name are you doing here?' "

So very often the world places a higher standard upon our Christianity than many Christians do. The world expects to see a man or a woman who is different. But too many Christian people today have been very anxious that everybody recognize they are as different as chalk from cheese in matters of doctrine, but they apparently are eager to impress upon the world that they are not a bit different in matters of practice. ". . . so did not I, . . ." said Nehemiah.

But I could apply that statement on a deeper level yet. Today there are practices, you know only too well, immoral practices which are not only overlooked but encouraged, which twenty years ago would have been frowned upon in all so-called Christian nations. There are things taking place between fellows and girls before marriage which are regarded today as the normal thing. In this country, in Britain, and in other so-called Christian lands there is a tremendous and alarming decline of moral standards. What was regarded as very wrong twenty years ago is now regarded as "the thing to do."

I want to ask you, what is your attitude toward all that? You may say you are horrified at it, but wait a moment! It is popular and it is the prevailing practice; perhaps unconsciously you have lowered the standard of your own moral life, of your moral thinking. In these last years, even in these last months, what about your own relationship with the opposite sex? Is it true that in your younger life you allowed things to happen before you were married that should not have happened, and now you face the future with a sense of shame?

I could tell you of great companies of educated young fellows and girls who go out from high school and college with a mother's prayers and a father's blessing and a church's great concern that they might be upright and clean-living Christian men and women. Yet they have been swept into the tide of this wretched, immoral business, and their lives have been ruined. Of course, they never intended it, they never meant it to happen, but they began by saying, "Just once, there's no harm in it, and it will never happen again. And because I'm young, of course I can stop when I like." That is the language of youth. That is the language of a man who thinks he is master of his own desires. Many a man has been humbled and brought low when too late he has recognized that he is a helpless slave to his own passions.

Do I speak to somebody who has lowered the standard? You know perfectly well that if you had to speak to your parents about it, you would be ashamed. Sometimes we notice a gap in church work, maybe among the Sunday school teachers, or maybe in the pastoral work, and sometimes a gap where a man once held an official position, and you ask him why.

The answer is that his health broke down; he could not stand the strain of the schedule. Of course that may be true. But the fact of the matter may be that there was a moment when he permitted self-indulgence and sin and avarice to get hold of him, saying it would never happen again, it was only an outlet for his personality, and there must be a time of self-expression—at that moment the man began to go down. Nehemiah said, ". . . so did not I."

I speak not only to young men and women but to those in middle life who perhaps have looked at something filthy and rotten, and have filled their minds with impurity and lust which have strangled their prayer life, smothered their Bible study and ruined their testimony. My friend, God has a word to say to you today about this. No one should dare take a position of leadership in Christian work unless he can look people in the face with a life that is above reproach and say, "So did not I." And there is nobody who could do that were it not that he was able to look back on days and years that have gone, and thank God for the blood of Jesus Christ that cleanses from all sin by the grace of a living God and the power of a Holy Spirit.

I am concerned also about people who have lowered the standard, perhaps, by bringing the movie-show into their homes, and using it behind the scenes as a kind of letdown. I am concerned, too, about fellows and girls who have never yet known the mutual joy of being united together in matrimony as husband and wife, but who know all about it before they have ever been there. I am concerned desperately about the boy and girl relationships in our high schools and college groups; things go on that are just not right, and they have just been letting go and allowing the enemy to drag down their standard of morality.

". . . so did not I," said this man Nehemiah. There is an attitude to maintain, but Nehemiah also had a motive to inspire him: ". . . so did not I," he said, "because of the fear of God." None can ever ascend unto the hill of the Lord except he has clean hands and a pure heart, for without holiness no man can see the Lord. And if we are going to stand before Him with clean hands and a pure heart, we will have to be

men and women who look up to Him with thanksgiving
that our lives have been made pure by the blood of Jesus
Christ.

We take the words of Nehemiah out from the Old Testament into the New, and as the only basis for holiness and
victory in my own life I have to say to you, "So did not I,
because of the love of Jesus." That is the only motive that
can inspire a man to stay right with God, to keep his life
pure and clean.

That He should be the sacrifice and be made sin that I
might be separated from that which ultimately would lead
me to hell, that He took it all into His own heart and into
His own body, that is the only motive which can make a
man holy and pure. Only the inexpressible love of Christ as
shown on the cross of Calvary can enable a man to refuse
the thing that would cause him to fall, to say, "No! Because
of what it cost God to save me, never!" Because of the love
of my Saviour I cannot look at the thing; because He loved
me so, I cannot indulge in that habit.

Your Christian experience is valueless, regardless of what
you believe, unless it leads you to a standard of conduct
which is in violent opposition to a lot that goes on in the
world today. The Saviour said there are two ways in which
a man may live: "Straight is the gate, therefore go in at it!
Narrow is the way that leads unto life, and few there be that
find it. Therefore, before it is too late, enter in. But," He
said, "wide is the gate, therefore stay out! Broad is the way;
keep clear—right about face and into the way that leads
to glory" (from Matthew 7:13, 14).

You will be unpopular and despised, but you will be
following in His steps. There are many people who do not

believe as you believe, and are not prepared to live as you would live, but in their hearts they will respect you for the courage to do it.

I want to remind you that a man may say, "I believe in Jesus; I believe in my Bible," but if you could look into his heart you would see there a cesspool. If you know perfectly well your relationships in your school and in your home life are tinged with immorality, and one day there will be someone who wishes they had never set eyes upon you, how dare you be a Christian minister or a Christian leader? I beg you today to get back to the cross and let the love of Jesus be your motive to inspire you to holy living.

There was an attitude to maintain, a motive to inspire, and also a power to overcome in Nehemiah's life.

Where do we find the power to overcome? It is found in the same place as the motive to inspire: the cross of Jesus Christ. In the cross there is not only the mighty inspiration of the love of God, but also the secret of dynamic power which can turn out sin and implant holiness in human lives. The cross is central and basic to holy living. Nobody can know what the victorious life is merely by going to Calvary to be forgiven; he must stay at Calvary until he knows something of the wounds in his own spirit, until he knows something of what it means for the Holy Spirit to crucify his lust, and his affections, and his desires. That life which was sacrificed upon the cross, that perfect life of purity which triumphed over the grave, is now at the disposal of every believer. For by the Holy Spirit He can enter into our hearts and live out His holiness in us. We cannot overcome, but He can! Under His authority we have the authority over the enemy.

". . . so did not I, because of the fear of God. Yea, also I continued in the work of this wall. . . ." The secret of triumph is found not only in saying "no" to sin but also in saying "yes" to God's will and purpose. Nehemiah went on with the positive, as well as refusing the negative. It is from the vantage ground of a life that is above suspicion that we can command respect and are able to take our place in Christian leadership. It is from that stand that God can make us a mighty weapon in His hand for blessing to others.

9. Total Christian Warfare

Now it came to pass, when Sanballat, and Tobiah, and Geshem the Arabian, and the rest of our enemies, heard that I had builded the wall, and that there was no breach left therein: (though at that time I had not set up the doors upon the gates;)

That Sanballat and Geshem sent unto me, saying, Come, let us meet together in some one of the villages in the plain of Ono. But they thought to do me mischief.

And I sent messengers unto them, saying, I am doing a great work, so that I cannot come down: why should the work cease, whilst I leave it, and come down to you?

Yet they sent unto me four times after this sort; and I answered them after the same manner.

Then sent Sanballat his servant unto me in like manner the fifth time with an open letter in his hand;

Wherein was written, It is reported among the heathen, and Gashmu saith it, that thou and the Jews think to rebel: for which cause thou buildest the wall, that thou mayest be their king, according to these words.

And thou hast also appointed prophets to preach of thee at Jerusalem, saying, There is a king in Judah: and now shall it be reported to the king according to these words. Come now therefore, and let us take counsel together.

Then I sent unto him, saying, There are no such things done as thou sayest, but thou feignest them out of thine own heart.

For they all made us afraid, saying, Their hands shall

be weakened from the work, that it be not done. Now therefore, O God, strengthen my hands.

Afterward I came unto the house of Shemaiah the son of Delaiah the son of Mehetabeel, who was shut up; and he said, Let us meet together in the house of God, within the temple, and let us shut the doors of the temple: for they will come to slay thee; yea, in the night will they come to slay thee.

And I said, Should such a man as I flee? and who is there, that being as I am, would go into the temple to save his life? I will not go in.

And, lo, I perceived that God had not sent him; but that he pronounced this prophecy against me: for Tobiah and Sanballat had hired him.

Therefore was he hired, that I should be afraid, and do so, and sin, and that they might have matter for an evil report, that they might reproach me.

My God, think thou upon Tobiah and Sanballat according to these their works, and on the prophetess Noadiah, and the rest of the prophets, that would have put me in fear.

So the wall was finished in the twenty and fifth day of the month Elul, in fifty and two days.

And it came to pass, that when all our enemies heard thereof, and all the heathen that were about us saw these things, they were much cast down in their own eyes: for they perceived that this work was wrought of our God.

Moreover in those days the nobles of Judah sent many letters unto Tobiah, and the letters of Tobiah came unto them.

For there were many in Judah sworn unto him, because he was the son in law of Shechaniah the son of Arah; and *his son Johanan had taken the daughter of Meshullam the son of Berechiah.*

Also they reported his good deeds before me, and uttered my words to him. And Tobiah sent letters to put me in fear.

—Nehemiah 6:1-19

THE VERY FIRST word of Nehemiah 6:15 is the most important one, because it sums up the work: "*So* the wall was finished." That word introduces us into the method by which this work of God, the building of the wall of Jerusalem, was brought to a triumphant conclusion. It gives us an insight into the heart of the man whom God used to see it through. It sounds the note of victory. It suggests the intensity of the conflict which had to be endured before the opposition was overthrown. "*So* the wall was finished."

There is a twofold explanation of the success of Nehemiah in the work to which God had called him. The first is in the sixteenth verse: ". . . this work was wrought of our God." The second is the subject of the whole chapter. There is always a twofold explanation for the success of any work of God. The one is divine, the other is human. The first is the fact that it is "wrought of God"; the second is total, unreserved human cooperation.

It is with the second of these that I want to deal mainly, but just a word about this divine explanation first of all. Nehemiah triumphed because he was doing a work which God initiated, and because God initiated it, God Himself empowered it. It would never have succeeded unless God had begun it; unless the origin of this work had been in the heart of God, it would never have been in the heart of Nehemiah. I would also remind you that we are not here to initiate programs for God or for His church. We are not here to initiate anything.

Our God has one great and burning passion upon His heart. It is to find a man here, another there, a girl here, another there, and so to fill them with His Holy Spirit that they may become channels through whom He can do what He plans to do. I repeat: we are not called upon to initiate programs; we are called to impart God's Spirit to the world and generation in which we live. The burden on the heart of God is for the multitude who are like sheep without a shepherd. I would dare to be so bold as to say that God cares for nothing else than that. Everything else is secondary.

He is not interested in our attempts at social reconstruction, or our desire to establish a new order of world peace, for God knows perfectly well that the only order that can ever succeed is the order which was given to regenerate men and women on the day of Pentecost. That is the only new order that can ever work, and the peace of God in the human heart is the only peace that can ever last.

God's great longing today is for the salvation of men from the world, the flesh, and the devil, before it is too late. The world in which we live is fast ripening for judgment, and there will come a moment when God's day of grace will end and His day of judgment will be inaugurated. The one great concern in the heart of the Father, the Son, and the Holy Spirit is to rescue dying men and to save them from an eternal hell before the judgment hour must strike.

In order to accomplish His purposes He deigns to use human agencies and human cooperation. He longs that every one of us may be usable. If we are not, that will not thwart God's purpose; it will only mean that we will be cast away and set aside in order that God may pick out one here and one there, all who are willing to cooperate with Him in the fulfillment of His purpose.

The great question is, how many people are taking the situation today seriously enough and personally enough to enable God to use them? It surely should be perfectly obvious to any thinking person that the powers which are operative in our modern age are far greater than mere human energy. It seems that world tension is constantly near the explosion point; the causes lie in human hearts, but they are inspired by satanic power. Atheistic, aggressive communism cannot be battled on any other level than that of bold, daring Christianity. There is an answer to the forces of evil only in the spiritual force of good. It is plain nonsense to attempt to defeat communism on the level of diplomacy and politics, because we are doomed to failure if we do. The one hope of our day is a militant church, totally abandoned to the will of God. For I believe that one day every one of us will be held accountable before God as to how we have or have not met the challenge of our day, whether or not we have lived our lives on such a level that we are totally available for God's holy purposes. If God does not find in His church today many such Christians, then we are jumping headlong to disaster. One thing, and one thing only can stem the tide, if it is the purpose of God to stem it and for Jesus not to come immediately: a mighty Holy Spirit-filled conviction on the part of God's people that we have the Light, and that our lives must be the demonstration of it.

God took hold of this man Nehemiah and found in him a man through whom He had a clear channel, "*So* the wall was finished." On the one hand, there was a plan initiated in heaven; on the other hand, there was a man totally abandoned to the will of God. Oh, to be like Nehemiah! Oh, to be found worthy of God's trust in these terrible days!

What is this cooperation for which God is asking? I believe it to be a determination to resist at all costs the onslaughts of Satan upon our lives and to go right through with the Saviour to the very end. At least, that is what I find in Nehemiah's autobiography here in chapter six. The wall was nearly finished. The opposition was crowding on full sail in a last-minute effort to prevent its completion. And whatever your views on prophecy may be, it must be the conviction of most of us that the war is nearly finished, the redemptive purposes of God in this day of grace are nearly completed, and we are living in the last days when Satan is putting on all possible effort to thwart the purpose of God.

What had Nehemiah to face? I want you to observe three forms of attack in chapter six which this man of God had to resist.

The first is the snare of the world's friendship. When the work had been in its earlier stages, ridicule, threatening, abuse and scorn had been the chief weapons of the enemy. But now that the work was almost complete, the enemy had abandoned scorn and abuse and had adopted a much more subtle line of attack. And in the second verse of this chapter we read that they came to Nehemiah four times with this request: "Come and let us meet together in the plain."

"Nehemiah, come down to our level. Don't be so extreme! Don't be so fanatical and bigoted! Don't be so narrow!"

Have you ever heard that language? Is it familiar to your ears? Have you heard whispered in your ear, "You've done your bit. Take it easy." That is always <u>one of Satan's</u> <u>methods of attack.</u> He is always saying "Come down," holding out fascinating bait, using all his craftiness to make the man of God compromise. You believe in a personal devil, of course, because you believe in a personal Saviour. Satan is not so concerned with you as a Christian unless, of course, you blunder badly in some moral issue. He is chiefly concerned to make you compromise. If he can persuade you on one issue to let down your standard of Christian conduct, to persuade you that "there's no harm in it," he has secured a major victory. He says, in effect, "Be a Christian if you like, but don't be fanatical about it. Let go those high principles, come down from that standard. It doesn't work, anyway. Retain your worldly friends and your worldly interests. Visit a show and go to a dance now and again. Keep a balanced mind—you'll go crazy if you don't, and get religious mania."

I would remind you that we have not received the spirit of bondage unto fear, but we have received the spirit ". . . of power, and of love, and of a sound mind" (<u>II Timothy</u> <u>1:7</u>). And <u>the only man or woman who is utterly sound in</u> <u>mind is the one who is giving to God an utter, one hundred</u> <u>per cent consecration of his life.</u> Any man who seeks to do a work for God is always being persuaded just in one thing to lower the standard, and herein lies the snare of the world's friendship.

Why is that? When a Christian compromises, at that moment he thwarts the power of the Third Person of the Trinity in his life. The great victories of the devil, I repeat, are not based on moral collapses in Christians—thank heaven they are few and far between—but when a man who takes a stand for separation and consecration is persuaded by someone or something to compromise in one detail, from that moment Satan has got him in his grip, and that man has become useless as a channel for the blessing of God. A compromising Christian is in God's way instead of being a blessing to humanity.

In the second place, in verses 5 to 7 observe that Nehemiah had to face the subtlety of the world's slander. See how they charged him with pride and with self-seeking: they said he was doing the thing for his own ends. He was planning to set up a kingdom of his own there in Jerusalem, they said.

If the world cannot persuade the Christian to compromise, it will begin to spread rumors about him and misrepresent his motives. If a Christian is all out for God and souls, he becomes a target for other people's tongues. And the worst enemy of Christian people is the last member of the human body to be consecrated: this thing in our mouth which one moment speaks love and the next moment venom. Few people give a man of God credit for speaking only to the glory of God. He must have an axe to grind! Even his character becomes the subject of gossip, and some man who has sought to live a pure, godly, holy life is brought down to shame because somebody has spread a rumor about him.

God forbid that any of us should be a tool in Satan's hands, and if we are tempted to talk scandal about another Christian, let us pray that God will set a watch over our lips. Whether you be a pastor or a teacher or evangelist or Sunday school leader, or whatever your position may be in Christian leadership, let me say that there will always be those who are friendly to your face, but who plan your downfall behind your back. Beware of the fawning, flattering Christian who is always fluttering around you, and who behind your back will be the first to rejoice when you go down. They will have their part in the fire which will never be quenched, for Jesus said, "Not every one that saith unto me, Lord, Lord, shall enter into the kingdom of heaven; but he that doeth the will of my Father which is in heaven" (Matthew 7:21).

In the third place, Nehemiah had to face, not only the snare of the world's friendship and the subtlety of the world's slander, but the scandal of the world's religion. In the tenth verse we read that one of the enemy, having failed at a pretense of friendship and having failed at slander, has now come as a wolf in sheep's clothing. We all believe that Satan is far less dangerous as a roaring lion than he is as an angel of light, and because he comes to us as an angel of light, we must stay on our guard at all times. This man professes to be a prophet, you notice, and he urges Nehemiah to flee and to shut himself up in the temple lest the enemy should slay him. He seeks to persuade Nehemiah into an easy-going, compromising religion that will shirk persecution, that will carry no cross, and that is governed by fear of the opinions of other people.

No man can lead a work of God if he allows himself to be governed by what other people think. He is to secure help, fellowship, prayer, advice, and he is foolish not to take it; but if his ultimate decisions are based upon popular opinion he is going to fail.

Here too is the worst form of intrigue, for among Nehemiah's own followers were those who were in correspondence with the enemy, writing letters, exchanging views, in alliance with the enemy. And why? Because of mixed marriages.

Now there are plenty of men in any church who know the right thing, but who often are afraid of petticoat government. They know what they should do, but they are persuaded by their life partner not to do it. And many a wife knows the stand she should take for God, uncompromising in her home, but she is afraid to do it because of what her husband might say. Many a man will have certain convictions regarding certain issues in his home, but he will refuse to go along with what he knows to be right because of the effect it might have upon his family, upon his children. I imagine that all of us know something about attacks along that line.

I am most concerned about this last point, the secret of the worker's success. Here is a man who succeeded, and by the grace of God I want to learn the lesson, and I trust you do, too. How thrilling it is! How did he answer the suggestion that he should come down—the snare of the world's friendship? "I am doing a great work, so that I cannot come down: why should the work cease, whilst I leave it, and come down to you?"

He faced the world's slander with an open denial of their accusations: "There are no such things done as thou sayest, but thou feignest them out of thine own heart. . . . O God, strengthen my hands."

He faced the scandal of the world's religion with a firm defiance: "Should such a man as I flee?"

But I would not win your hearts nor win your response if I were to point you only to Nehemiah. He is but a type, a shadow. Do you see Christ in your open Bible every time

you read it? From Genesis 1 to Revelation 22 it will tell
you about Him if you look for Him. Some books in the
Bible do not even mention Him; for example, the Book of
Proverbs never says anything about the Lord, but if when
you read it, instead of "wisdom" put in the word "Christ,"
and the whole book will begin to live for you, for "He is
made unto you wisdom." And here in Nehemiah what a
wonderful picture we have of our precious Lord! Nehemiah
is the shadow: Christ Himself is the reality.

God had only one way of fulfilling His redemptive plan
to save your soul from hell, and that was to secure the utter
cooperation of His well-beloved Son who had been with
Him since before time was. And the Lord Jesus, in order to
be the vehicle through whom God could fulfill our redemption, had to face exactly what Nehemiah had to face. "Come
down and meet with us in the plain," said Nehemiah's
enemies. And the crowd jeered at Christ and they spat upon
Him and mocked Him as He hung upon a cross, "If thou
be the Son of God, come down."

We hear the echo of Nehemiah's words, "I cannot come
down; I am doing a great work." "He saved others, himself
he could not save." And what a work! If He had come
down, there would not have been salvation for one single
individual, and the whole world would have been plunged
into an eternal hell. Jesus said, in effect, "No, I cannot and
will not come down, for then nobody will be saved."

We are His representatives, and I want to remind you that
we are, in God's sight, seated with Christ in heavenly places,
high above all principalities and powers. Should we come
down to this world that is under judgment? No, indeed! Is

that your answer to the snare of the world's friendship? Jesus said, "No," and in His name will you say, "No"?

They slandered Him: He not only faced the snare of the world's friendship but the subtlety of the world's slander. They said He was a gluttonous man and a winebibber. They said He was a friend of sinners. They misrepresented His motives over and over again. They accused Him falsely. But when He was reviled, He reviled not again. Someone has been slandering your reputation and talking about you critically and unkindly. Will you answer back, or can you, by the grace of God, take it in Jesus' name?

He also had to face the scandal of the world's religion. The devil sought to keep Him from the cross, to persuade Him to take the easy way. But though He could have called twelve legions of angels to His aid, He refused to flee. And at the end of it all He was able to say, "*So* the work is done!"

How far are we willing to cooperate with the Lord in seeing His work through to a finish? The Holy Spirit wants to fill us with the love of Jesus, for only then can He use us. He wants to light the flame of Calvary-love in our hearts for the lost. He wants us to share His vision, share His burden, and regardless of public opinion and popularity, He wants men and women who will go all the way with Him. Are you thus finishing the work?

10. Strength for the Battle

And all the people gathered themselves together as one man into the street that was before the water gate; and they spake unto Ezra the scribe to bring the book of the law of Moses, which the Lord had commanded to Israel.

And Ezra the priest brought the law before the congregation both of men and women, and all that could hear with understanding, upon the first day of the seventh month.

And he read therein before the street that was before the water gate from the morning until midday, before the men and the women, and those that could understand; and the ears of all the people were attentive unto the book of the law.

And Ezra the scribe stood upon a pulpit of wood, which they had made for the purpose; and beside him stood Mattithiah, and Shema, and Anaiah, and Urijah, and Hilkiah, and Maaseiah, on his right hand; and on his left hand, Pedaiah, and Mishael, and Malchiah, and Hashum, and Hashbadana, Zechariah, and Meshullam.

And Ezra opened the book in the sight of all the people; (for he was above all the people;) and when he opened it, all the people stood up:

And Ezra blessed the Lord, the great God. And all the people answered, Amen, Amen, with lifting up their hands: and they bowed their heads, and worshipped the Lord with their faces to the ground.

Also Jeshua, and Bani, and Sherebiah, Jamin, Akkub, Shabbethai, Hodijah, Maaseiah, Kelita, Azariah, Jozabad,

Hanan, Pelaiah, and the Levites, caused the people to understand the law: and the people stood in their place.

So they read in the book in the law of God distinctly, and gave the sense, and caused them to understand the reading.

And Nehemiah, which is the Tirshatha, and Ezra the priest the scribe, and the Levites that taught the people, said unto all the people, This day is holy unto the Lord your God; mourn not, nor weep. For all the people wept, when they heard the words of the law.

Then he said unto them, Go your way, eat the fat, and drink the sweet, and send portions unto them for whom nothing is prepared: for this day is holy unto our Lord: neither be ye sorry; for the joy of the Lord is your strength.

So the Levites stilled all the people, saying, Hold your peace, for the day is holy; neither be ye grieved.

And all the people went their way to eat, and to drink, and to send portions, and to make great mirth, because they had understood the words that were declared unto them.

—Nehemiah 8:1-12

As we observed in our opening chapter, the Book of Nehemiah is really divided into two parts. The first six chapters tell us of the reconstruction of the walls of Jerusalem; the last seven chapters have to do with the re-instruction of the people of God. It is to this second part that we turn now, in the seventh and eighth chapters of Nehemiah.

His great task, the rebuilding of the ruined wall around Jerusalem, having been completed, Nehemiah fades out of the picture for the moment. Ezra the scribe steps on the scene here. He has been back in Jerusalem some thirteen years longer than Nehemiah, and he has been right alongside him all the time the wall was being built.

The completion of the wall of Jerusalem marked a tremendous victory and a great achievement, but it was no moment for relaxation on the part of the builders. In fact, this was a moment of supreme peril. Throughout all the country surrounding that city were enemies of the people of God, eager to attack them in spite of the wall. Because of them Jerusalem would be in perpetual danger.

It is ever true that the great moment of achievement or success in Christian work is perhaps one of the most dangerous moments in a man's life. Joshua discovered that fact, as you may remember. The tremendous triumph at Jericho was followed by a tragic and humiliating defeat at Ai simply because the power of the enemy was underestimated. The people of God imagined that their great achievement at

Jericho—which was really not their own at all, but entirely God's—had imparted to them some peculiar inherent strength for future battles.

Are we not always in exactly the same peril? It is easy to imagine that, to quote the words of a wonderful old hymn—yet daring to suggest that it is not too accurate— "Each victory will help you some other to win."

There is no experience in our Christian life, no matter how exhilarating or triumphant, which imparts to us strength for the future. It leaves us just as poor and helpless and needy as before, but for the grace of God and the power of the blood of Jesus.

To glance through chapters seven and eight of Nehemiah is to recognize how fully alert both Ezra and Nehemiah were to this principle. They made very careful provision about the opening and closing of the city gate, and set up rules for those who would be on duty as watchers. They were determined to be on their guard against possible attack.

Is it not true that faith and presumption are poles apart? To be careless in spiritual things and to underestimate satanic power is never a sign of piety or of extreme bravery, but rather of complete folly. Every alert soldier of the cross will always be prepared for the possibility of a counterattack from the devil, and will make it a principle of his life to watch and pray.

You will notice the type of man whom Nehemiah chose to put in charge of the city. He is described in the seventh chapter and the second verse as "a faithful man," and one who "feared God above many"—faithfulness and fidelity. Hanani was evidently a man whom Nehemiah felt he could trust anywhere. That is the kind of person we need in

Christian work. How many of us loudly proclaim our loyalty to God while we are desperately unfaithful to the task
given to us in His service! Reverent fear of God is the key
to faithfulness in any situation.

At this moment of achievement, therefore, there was
nothing more necessary than that the people of God should
be brought to an intelligent understanding of the Word of
God, and to a spiritual understanding of the secret of their
strength for the future. The chapter from which this particular text is chosen recounts the holding of a quite remarkable convention (a convention, I may say, as distinct
from a conference—a conference being a place for discus-
sion, a convention a place for decision). You will observe
that the people gathered together as one man to hear the
Word of God. It was not only read to them, but expounded,
distinctly and clearly.

The result was that the people were made conscious of
their own failure and sin, and they wept. What an amazing
thing! This day of great victory was also a day of deep conviction resulting in sadness of heart as they discovered how
serious had been their failure in the light of God's Word.

But does not this always happen in those who walk with
God in the light of His Word? Every progressive taste of
the fruit of Calvary in our lives, and of the power of the
risen Lord, is accompanied by an increasing revelation of
our own corruption. God never allows us to get away with
the idea that we are becoming progressively good and
holy. Always He seeks to remind us that He will not give
His glory to another, that the battle is His and the victory
is His. To say, as Paul did, that ". . . in me (that is, in my
flesh,) dwelleth no good thing . . ." (Romans 7:18), if it is

said with utter sincerity, is a great step forward in the
spirit of true discernment.

But if it be true that we are utterly helpless, how is the
battle to be won? What is the secret of strength? Where can
power be found to avoid the failures and shortcomings of
the past?

The answer of Ezra and Nehemiah was simply this, "The
joy of the Lord is your strength."

Now, I am sure that there are many of us, only too conscious of failure of one kind or another, who would give a
great deal to discover the secret of strength for the future.
We have wept and mourned over our sins, and we go on
doing so, yet somehow the failure is still there. We are all
conscious of the need of a strength which is enduring, not
just a little increase in power for a moment, but real stamina
which will endure for all our lives.

A spirit of conviction is a very wonderful thing, when a
heart is broken in recognition of its own complete failure.
But do you know, the devil can use even that to his own
ends? What a subtle foe he is! He is far too strong for us.
Only by leaning upon the Lord can we overcome him con-
sistently. When a deep spirit of conviction of the Spirit of
God comes to us, and we see our breakdown and failure and
sins in the light of the Word of God, we may be tempted to
feel, "It's no use. I might as well forget it altogether. I am
just a hopeless sinner, and I might as well give in." That's
what Satan likes to say to us! When he has caused us in
some particular issue to fail, he then whispers to us, "I told
you so—this Christian life is no use. You can't live it." Having got us down, there is nothing he likes more than to
keep us down.

But true conviction of the Holy Spirit is not intended for that—of course not. It is intended to bring us to the end of our own strength that we might discover infinite resources in Christ our Lord.

I have known Christian people who have been conscious of sin in their lives and have almost given up praying, assuming that there was no real victory for them in some particular battlefront in life. They have been horrified to discover the evil in their own hearts. But it is always a great comfort to me to recognize that the things that shock me about myself never shock God. He knew all about them before He undertook my salvation. There was not a potential sin in my heart which He did not see and of which He was not fully aware. It may surprise us to discover how basically and inherently sinful we are, but it certainly does not surprise Him, and He has adequate resources to meet our need.

What are these resources? Once again let us listen to the Word of the Lord through Ezra to a people that were bowed down under conviction. ". . . Go your way, eat the fat, and drink the sweet, and send portions unto them for whom nothing is prepared: for this day is holy unto our Lord: neither be ye sorry; for the joy of the Lord is your strength" (8:10).

What is the joy of the Lord? What is this which Ezra claimed was to be the strength of the people? Certainly it is not hilarity, not the hollow laughter of the world nor cheap emotion. It is something infinitely deeper than that.

In the first place, I would suggest to you that it is joy based upon forgiveness. We are not forgiven because we are sorry for sin: the only explanation for the forgiveness of God is found in the death of Christ. No matter who or what we are, there is absolute acceptance before God by the death of His Son, and by no other way. Forgiveness is not something that we earn; it is something we accept as His gift. All our pleading which refuses to recognize the cross as the basis of forgiveness is of no avail. It is battering at another door altogether from the one which Jesus has opened through His sacrifice.

So many people say, "I do not want to come to God that way. It is so humiliating to be received as a sinner." But the Word of God answers with all heavenly authority, ". . . there is none other name under heaven given among men, whereby we must be saved" (Acts 4:12). And there are not two ways, but only one way. What you might think is heartlessness on the part of God is indeed the expression of His real heart, for there is limitless entrance by His way. Once we have come that way, then the joy of the Lord has begun, for we have been forgiven.

The prodigal son was once starving in a far country, but when he went back home he was clothed with the best robe and a ring was put on his finger, precious symbols indeed of God's forgiving mercy. He had been alone in the far country, but at home not he only, but "they" began to be merry.

This indeed was the joy of the Lord, based upon forgiveness: the knowledge that the past has been dealt with righteously and is covered by the precious blood of Christ. "There is therefore now no condemnation to them which are in Christ Jesus . . ." (Romans 8:1).

When God forgives, He forgets, casting all our sins into the depths of the sea, behind His back, as far as the east is from the west—what amazing expressions the Word of God uses to assure us on this point! Therefore why should we allow Satan to drag up before our minds that which is put away forever out of the mind of God? This is one real secret of joy.

Then I would say the second secret of the joy of the Lord is that it is nourished in affliction. You see, a Christian is one who should always be rejoicing. Not that he goes around saying, "Hallelujah, brother!" all the time! Noise is not always an evidence of spirituality. But he should possess rather a calm, quiet serenity in every situation.

When you see somebody like that, you say automatically to yourself, "It is all very well for him to be joyous. He doesn't know anything about problems like mine. He has no burdens."

Hasn't he? Just lift the veil from that life, if you could, and you would discover that the fact that the joy is there is a sure sign that the burden is there, too. The burden which God places in a life means that the grape is being squeezed and crushed, and out comes the wine. Most of us see only the wine of joy, not realizing that behind the joy is the pressure of trial.

Such a man will not talk about it. He does not go around looking for sympathy; he is delivered from self-pity. It is something essentially between himself and his Lord, something which others cannot share, because it is the whole strength of his life.

Do you question that? Then I suggest that you do some of the visitation which it is my privilege to do from time to time, and you would soon know. I am more than humbled when I leave some homes where I have discovered, in a life which seemed so radiant and joyful, an affliction, a very

deep affliction which is being borne so triumphantly that
the joy of the Lord is revealed through it.

Take a look for a moment at the life of our Lord. What a
burden He bore! None was so afflicted as He, "a man of
sorrows and acquainted with grief," yet He says, "These
things have I spoken unto you, that my joy might remain
in you, and that your joy might be full" (John 15:11).

Then a third secret of the joy of the Lord is, I think, that
it is dependent upon obedience to God and not upon successful Christian service.

The joy of the Lord—just think of that for a moment.
The Lord Jesus, ". . . who for the joy that was set before
him endured the cross, despising the shame . . ." as the
writer to the Hebrews tells us (12:2)—the secret of His
joy lay in doing what the Father had sent Him to do.

Judged on a purely human level, it would seem that the
result of His ministry was a failure. How few people He
gathered around Himself! In fact, His whole ministry was
rejected, but He pressed on, through all the shame of the
cross, for the joy that was set before Him. Doing the will
of God, obeying the command of God—these are the
things which bring joy.

That means, of course, that you are prepared to be
counted as a failure in the eyes of other people. I am sure
you have discovered in the course of life that there is very
little charity among many Christian folk. They are prepared
to excuse the worldling quite a lot, but they will never
excuse the Christian for failure in Christian work. He must
produce results; he must get decisions; he must be a success.
The Lord may graciously give us results and grant us a
mighty wave of blessing, but He may choose to withhold

it; that is entirely in His hand. The one thing that matters in any sphere of service is that you are doing the will of God, and that you are obedient to His word in the power of His Spirit. If that be true, then in your heart there will always be a deep joy.

I wonder if the joy bells are ringing in your heart as you read this? Do you leap to work or do you creep to it? Do you enjoy it or do you endure it? Yes, the joy of the Lord is based upon forgiveness, it is nourished in affliction, and it is dependent upon obedience.

But one other thing which needs to be said is this, that the joy of the Lord is independent of circumstances. The Christian knows, or should know, that no experience in life can ever touch him except by the permission of the Lord Himself. It is He who suffers us to be tested, but never beyond what we are able to bear, and with the testing—not before it or after it, but with it, always on time—He provides the way of escape. Testing or temptation, whatever you like to call it, will always be woven into the pattern of every Christian life. It is part of the will of God. Do not let us seek to shirk it.

Whatever God permits to touch our lives, we may be sure He will bestow power to see us through. The great question to ask in time of affliction is not "why?" but "what?" Not, "Why do these things happen?" but "What lesson does the Lord want me to learn in the midst of it all?" For in this respect we are all in a school from which we will never graduate until we get to heaven.

Therefore joy can enable us to sing in the night, just as Paul and Silas sang in prison. That does not mean, of course, that the Christian is always happy, for happiness depends on what happens. But it does mean that even in the midst of the heartbreak, deep down in his heart there is a joy that nothing on earth can ever take away.

Yes, the joy of the Lord can sing in times of self-efface-ment, as John the Baptist did when he said, ". . . the friend of the bridegroom . . . rejoiceth greatly because of the bridegroom's voice: this my joy therefore is fulfilled. He must increase, but I must decrease" (John 3:29, 30). It is not easy to keep rejoicing when you seem to be put on the shelf, or when you are never thanked or appreciated. But why should you be? The Lord Jesus never was. We soon lose our joy when we begin to look for recognition from other people. It is the joy of the Lord that makes us able to sing in temptation, to ". . . count it all joy when you fall into divers temptations," as James says (1:2), to remember that the Lord Jesus said, "Blessed are ye, when men shall . . . reproach you, and cast out your name as evil, for the Son of man's sake. Rejoice ye in that day, and leap for joy . . ." (Luke 6:22, 23).

The joy of the Lord means, in other words, that our eyes must be off ourselves and on the Lord Jesus, all the time. As someone has said, somewhat tritely, "The secret of joy is just J—O—Y, in that order: Jesus, Others, Yourself."

Let me add and underline the fact that this is not some-thing you can work up, but something that the Lord imparts to His children. It is a fruit of the Spirit, safely nestling in between love and peace in the great ninefold cluster of fruit in Galatians 5:22, 23. Let Him fill you, and joy will be as natural as the murmur of a stream as it flows. And remember, that joy will always reveal itself to other people.

As our text says, you will desire to send portions to those

for whom nothing is prepared. There is nothing so contagious as a joyful Christian. His joy can bring such a benediction into sad and weary hearts around him, as well as being the secret of strength for the battle of everyday living.

> Jesus, Thou joy of loving hearts,
> Thou fount of life, Thou light of men,
> From the best bliss that earth imparts
> We turn unfilled to Thee again.

11. Some Principles of Revival

Now in the twenty and fourth day of this month the children of Israel were assembled with fasting, and with sackclothes, and earth upon them.

And the seed of Israel separated themselves from all strangers, and stood and confessed their sins, and the iniquities of their fathers.

And they stood up in their place, and read in the book of the law of the Lord their God one fourth part of the day; and another fourth part they confessed, and worshipped the Lord their God.

Then stood up upon the stairs, of the Levites, Jeshua, and Bani, Kadmiel, Shebaniah, Bunni, Sherebiah, Bani, and Chenani, and cried with a loud voice unto the Lord their God.

Then the Levites, Jeshua, and Kadmiel, Bani, Hashabniah, Sherebiah, Hodijah, Shebaniah, and Pethahiah, said, Stand up and bless the Lord your God for ever and ever: and blessed be thy glorious name, which is exalted above all blessing and praise.

Thou, even thou, art Lord alone; thou hast made heaven, the heaven of heavens, with all their host, the earth, and all things that are therein, the seas, and all that is therein, and thou preservest them all; and the host of heaven worshippeth thee.

Thou art the Lord the God, who didst choose Abram, and broughtest him forth out of Ur of the Chaldees, and gavest him the name of Abraham;

And foundest his heart faithful before thee, and madest

a covenant with him to give the land of the Canaanites, the Hittites, the Amorites, and the Perizzites, and the Jebusites, and the Girgashites, to give it, I say, to his seed, and hast performed thy words; for thou art righteous:

And didst see the affliction of our fathers in Egypt, and heardest their cry by the Red sea;

And shewedst signs and wonders upon Pharaoh, and on all his servants, and on all the people of his land: for thou knewest that they dealt proudly against them. So didst thou get thee a name, as it is this day.

And thou didst divide the sea before them, so that they went through the midst of the sea on the dry land; and their persecutors thou threwest into the deeps, as a stone into the mighty waters.

Moreover thou leddest them in the day by a cloudy pillar; and in the night by a pillar of fire, to give them light in the way wherein they should go.

Thou camest down also upon mount Sinai, and spakest with them from heaven, and gavest them right judgments, and true laws, good statutes and commandments:

And madest known unto them thy holy sabbath, and commandedst them precepts, statutes, and laws, by the hand of Moses thy servant:

And gavest them bread from heaven for their hunger, and broughtest forth water for them out of the rock for their thirst, and promisedst them that they should go in to possess the land which thou hadst sworn to give them.

But they and our fathers dealt proudly, and hardened their necks, and hearkened not to thy commandments,

And refused to obey, neither were mindful of thy wonders that thou didst among them; but hardened their necks, and in their rebellion appointed a captain to return to their bondage: but thou art a God ready to pardon, gracious and merciful, slow to anger, and of great kindness, and forsookest them not.

Yea, when they had made them a molten calf, and said, This is thy God that brought thee up out of Egypt, and had wrought great provocations;

Yet thou in thy manifold mercies forsookest them not it the wilderness: the pillar of the cloud departed not from them by day, to lead them in the way; neither the pillar of fire by night, to shew them light, and the way wherein they should go.

Thou gavest also thy good spirit to instruct them, and withheldest not thy manna from their mouth, and gavest them water for their thirst.

Yea, forty years didst thou sustain them in the wilderness, so that they lacked nothing; their clothes waxed not old, and their feet swelled not.

Now therefore, our God, the great, the mighty, and the terrible God, who keepest covenant and mercy, let not all the trouble seem little before thee, that hath come upon us, on our kings, on our princes, and on our priests, and on our prophets, and on our fathers, and on all thy people, since the time of the kings of Assyria unto this day.

Howbeit thou art just in all that is brought upon us; for thou hast done right, but we have done wickedly:

Neither have our kings, our princes, our priests, nor our fathers, kept thy law, nor hearkened unto thy commandments and thy testimonies, wherewith thou didst testify against them.

For they have not served thee in their kingdom, and in thy great goodness that thou gavest them, and in the large and fat land which thou gavest before them, neither turned they from their wicked works.

Behold, we are servants this day, and for the land that thou gavest unto our fathers to eat the fruit thereof and the good thereof, behold, we are servants in it:

And it yieldeth much increase unto the kings whom thou hast set over us because of our sins: also they have dominion over our bodies, and over our cattle, at their pleasure, and we are in great distress.

And because of all this we make a sure covenant, and write it; and our princes, Levites, and priests, seal unto it.

—Nehemiah 9:1-21, 32-38

The days which followed the rebuilding of the wall of Jerusalem were like heaven on earth. Everything went right. It is quite tragic that the experience of blessing was short-lived; the reason for subsequent decline is given to us in the closing chapters of the Book of Nehemiah, to which we will come later. But we will be repaid now by looking at some of the great principles of revival displayed here, and recognizing that we may learn from this record how to avoid the pitfalls into which these people stumbled.

God is just the same today, and I believe He is just as eager to give us the fullness of His blessing. He never withholds it for any capricious reason of His own heart, but only waits for those of us who love Him to follow certain clearly defined principles in His Word. When we pray for revival, perhaps He does not answer because we do not follow these principles.

Of course, I would always distinguish revival from evangelism. Although often confused, the two are entirely different. Evangelism is winning the unsaved; revival has to do with the Christian. Evangelism is the permanent duty of the church; revival is a gracious outpouring of the Spirit of God.

It is possible to have a measure of success in evangelism without ever having revival, but I do believe that genuine revival in the church would lead to a mighty blessing in evangelism, inevitably.

The fact that the fruit of evangelistic witness today may be relatively small in comparison with the effort and money that are put into it is not necessarily the fault of the evangelist. To introduce young converts into dead churches, even though many of them are orthodox in doctrine, is to quench the Spirit and freeze out the fruit of a soul-saving ministry. We thank God for all the great evangelistic campaigns of Billy Graham and others, but how much more fruitful they would be if there were a revival of Christianity in depth in the lives of countless thousands of professing Christians in our churches.

Well might we cry to God:

> O Breath of Life, come sweeping through us,
> Revive Thy Church with life and power;
> O Breath of Life, come, cleanse, renew us,
> And fit Thy Church to meet this hour.
>
> O Wind of God, come bend us, break us,
> Till humbly we confess our need;
> Then in Thy tenderness remake us,
> Revive, restore, for this we plead.
>
> O Breath of Love, come breathe within us,
> Renewing thought and will and heart;
> Come, Love of Christ, afresh to win us,
> Revive Thy Church in every part.
>
> O Heart of Christ, once broken for us,
> 'Tis there we find our strength and rest;
> Our broken contrite hearts now solace,
> And let Thy waiting Church be blest.

Revive us, Lord! Is zeal abating
While harvest fields are vast and white?
Revive us, Lord, the world is waiting,
Equip Thy Church to spread the light.

—Bessie P. Head

As we seek out the principles of such an outpouring illustrated in this chapter, the principles of revival, we need to ask ourselves quite frankly if we are willing to have these four principles applied to our own lives and to our own church.

The first one is a return to brokenheartedness. It is found in the first two verses of chapter nine, "Now in the twenty and fourth day of this month the children of Israel were assembled with fasting, and with sackclothes, and earth upon them. And the seed of Israel separated themselves from all strangers, and stood and confessed their sins, and the iniquities of their fathers."

The wall had been rebuilt. The law of God had been expounded, as we read in the previous chapter. The feast of tabernacles, the harvest festival of the Jewish people, had been observed again for the first time since Joshua's day. The sixteenth verse of the eighth chapter says, "And there was very great gladness."

But after only a few days' interval, feasting gave place to fasting; joy became humiliation. Are we surprised at that? Is it not true that feasting—that is to say, fellowship, communion, rejoicing in the Lord—and fasting—that is to say, the denying of ourselves, humiliation of self—go together in Christian experience? They are constantly being repeated, they are constantly together.

Confessions of sin and repentance are not things to be

left in the background of Christian life, things that were only connected with the early days of Christian experience —far from it. It is the humble and contrite heart which God does not despise. It is the proud whom He knoweth afar off. If you avoid in your present Christian life a daily humiliation before God, you will soon become hardhearted, cold and indifferent to the things of God.

God will never plant the seed of His life upon the soil of a hard, unbroken spirit. He will only plant that seed where the conviction of His Spirit has brought brokenness, where the soil has been watered with the tears of repentance as well as the tears of joy. Days of great joy in the Lord are always accompanied by days of great humiliation in ourselves. How often the discovery of something new in the loveliness of the Lord Jesus has brought with it the discovery of some new corruption in our own hearts.

Christian people have too often relegated experiences like that to the early days of conversion. Oh, for that tenderness of heart that was ours when first we knew the Lord! How easily possible it is, in the pressure of life and business and Christian activity, for the grace of repentance to be just a memory! Oh, that God would give to us a renewal of brokenness to His will, and brokenness in our fellowship with others, in which there is a yieldedness to Him and to other Christians so that God can truly bless us!

If you want revival, let me remind you that God only plants the seed of His life in a soil which has been broken up by repentance. One principle of revival is brokenness of heart.

A second principle of revival in this chapter is a reflection upon God's goodness. Practically the whole of this ninth

chapter of Nehemiah is devoted to the prayer that the
people offered. What an utterance of praise there is here, and
what a confession of sin and failure! There is praise for what
God is, for His covenant with them through Abraham,
for His deliverance from Egyptian bondage, for His
tender guidance all during their history. In spite of all that,
there had been repeated sin and failure. And again and again
that failure was matched by a new outpouring of the
grace of God. I would recommend that you go through this
whole prayer in detail.

As the people counted their blessings one by one, they
found them to be innumerable. You will notice the constant
repetition, for instance, in verses 6-15, of that little con-
nective "and," as they reflect upon God's goodness.

"... *and* thou preservest them all ...
Thou ... didst choose Abram
and broughtest him forth out of Ur of the Chaldees,
and gavest him the name of Abraham ...
and madest a covenant with him ...
And didst see the affliction of our fathers in Egypt,
and heardest their cry by the Red sea;
And shewedst signs and wonders upon Pharaoh ...
And thou didst divide the sea before them ...
and their persecutors thou threwest into the deeps ...
Moreover thou leddest them in the day by a cloudy pillar;
and in the night by a pillar of fire ...
and spakest with them from heaven ...
And madest known unto them thy holy sabbath ...
and broughtest forth water for them out of the rock ...
and promisedst them that they should go in to possess the
    land. ..."

What a constant repetition of God's faithfulness, God's
goodness, God's grace, God's blessing!

Then note the word "but" in verse 16. In spite of all His goodness, how stubborn they were, how unyielded, how proud. "*But* they and our fathers dealt proudly . . . *but* thou art a God ready to pardon . . . Yea, when they had made a molten calf . . . Yet thou in thy manifold mercies forsookest them not in the wilderness. . . ."

The next verses go on to say again what God did for them in spite of all their rebellion. "Thou gavest also thy good spirit to instruct them, *and* withheldest not thy manna from their mouth. . . ."

And down to verse 26: "Nevertheless they were disobedient. . . . Therefore thou deliveredest them into the hand of their enemies. . . . But after they had rest, they did evil again before thee . . . yet when they returned, and cried unto thee, thou heardest them from heaven. . . . And testified against them, that thou mightest bring them again unto thy law: yet they dealt proudly . . ." (9:26-29).

"Yet many years didst thou forbear them, and testifiedst against them by thy spirit in thy prophets: yet would they not give ear: therefore gavest thou them into the hand of the people of the lands. Nevertheless for thy great mercies' sake thou didst not utterly consume them, nor forsake them; for thou art a gracious and a merciful God. Now therefore, our God, the great, the mighty and the terrible God . . . let not all the trouble seem little before thee, that hath come upon us . . ." (9:30-32).

Is not that the story of God's grace and God's goodness to us all? Is it not the story of our rebellion and indifference and coldness toward God? And God to them was so distant, and for us He is so near. He was outside them—He is inside us. There is less excuse for us than for them.

Do you ever take time for a reflection upon God's goodness?

In chapter nine in the third verse we are told that they spent three hours in the Word of God and three hours in prayer and worship—three hours in heart-searching and three hours in worship. It takes time for that spirit of prayer to get hold of people.

Just suppose you and I could take one day and do just that: lay down our tasks and show the Lord for one day that fellowship with Him was more important than anything else in the world. Just suppose you took time to reflect on God's goodness and to go back over the story of your life, the milestones past which He has led you, the path along which He has brought you. What a blessing it would be to reflect upon His goodness! I think we could come to the conclusion that God's mercy with a sinner is only equalled and perhaps outmatched by His patience with the saints, with you and me.

One principle of revival is taking time for reflection upon God's goodness, upon His way with you through the years that have passed. Have you done that lately?

> Oh, the pure delight of a single hour
> That before the throne I spend.

It is not up to me to ask you this question, but I pray that the Holy Spirit will. How long is it since you have spent a single hour alone with God?

The third principle of revival here is a recognition of our sinfulness. You will notice in the thirty-third verse of chapter nine, "Howbeit thou art just in all that is brought upon us; for thou hast done right, but we have done wickedly."

You see, in spite of the fact that they were back in the land, back in Jerusalem, they were only what you would call a "satellite" country. They were under the very ruthless dominion of Persia, and were just servants, as verse 38 says: "Behold, we are servants this day"—this people that were born to be free and liberated had to say, "We are today just servants because of the way we have lived."

It is a tremendous moment in a Christian's life when he can honestly look up into the face of God and say, "Yes, Lord, You are right and I am wrong," when he stops arguing with God, and drops his controversy. He says, "Lord, yes. I've got what I deserved in this situation. You are right; I am wrong." That is the thing for which God has been working in your life and mine from the very moment of our conversion.

I believe that God is more ready to forgive the sins of His people than a mother is to snatch a little child out of the fire, but the sin God never forgives is the sin we will not confess. That is why revival does not come.

People ask me constantly, "Pastor, what is the unforgivable sin?"

I have only the one answer, "The sin you won't confess." You can go through twenty years of life, perhaps, covering it up, refusing to recognize sinfulness.

There is no revival possible in any fellowship without a price being paid. Where sin has been open against the people of God, it has to be confessed openly. Where it has been against another, then it has to be confessed to that person. Where it has been against God, then it has to be confessed to Him, and all sin is against God.

To look up into the face of God and say, "Lord Jesus,

in this battle that we have fought, You have been right, and now I admit that I have been wrong," that is the end of controversy and the beginning of revival.

Some time ago at an all night of prayer in my church I read a list I use myself called "Self-examination questions," because I am desperately concerned in my own life on these things. I want to give this list to you, lest you think it is a comfortable, easy sort of business, this recognition of sin:

What about my relationship with men?

Am I consciously or unconsciously creating the impression that I am a better man than I really am? Is there the least suspicion of hypocrisy in my life? Am I honest in all my words and acts? Do I exaggerate?

Am I reliable? Can I be trusted? Do I confidentially pass on what was told to me in confidence? Do I grumble and complain in the church?

Am I jealous, impure, irritable, touchy, distrustful? Am I self-conscious, self-pitying, or self-justifying? Am I proud? Do I thank God I am not as other people? Is there anyone I fear, or dislike, or criticize, or resent? If so, what am I doing about it?

What about my devotion to God?

Does the Bible live to me? Do I give it time to speak to me? Do I go to bed in time and do I get up in time?

Am I enjoying my prayer life today? Did I enjoy it this morning? When I am involved in a problem in life, do I use my tongue or my knees about it?

Am I disobeying God in anything, or insisting upon doing something about which my conscience is very uneasy?

When did I last speak to someone else with the object of trying to win him for Christ?

Am I a slave to books, dress, friends, work, or convention? How do I spend my spare time?

I put those questions to myself constantly, and I find them very heart-searching. Have you thought about recognizing sinfulness lately? *That* is the price of revival.

The other principle of revival outlined for us here is the renewal of our obedience. In chapter ten you will see a covenant which the people made with God. Now the fact that they soon broke it should never discourage us from a similar sacred covenant. In the Old Testament the obedience of God's people was impelled by law, whereas ours is inspired by love. I want you to notice that the obedience of God's people touched every part of their lives: their home life, their social life, and their church life.

Revival is not simply an emotional upheaval—it leads to action. It causes the flower of love to blossom in the heart; it makes the river of God flow when it has been dry; it makes the desert burst into bloom.

"They clave to their brethren, their nobles, and entered into a curse, and into an oath, to walk in God's law, which was given by Moses the servant of God, and to observe and do all the commandments of the Lord our Lord, and his judgments and his statutes"—a renewal of obedience, here —"And that we would not give our daughters unto the people of the land, nor take their daughters for our sons" (10:29, 30).

That is to say, they restored the family altar that had broken down. How many altars are in desperate need of repair? Revival starts right there. When I restore the altar of the Lord, bring back discipline to my home life and renew a religious observance with my wife and family, I glorify God.

It affected social life as well as home life (v. 30). It meant

a clear line of separation as far as friendships were concerned, in which God's will came first and everything else
was secondary. Are you observing that today, young people,
or are you in danger of the unequal yoke?

In the third place it affects church life (v. 39). How
wonderfully this chapter closes: ". . . we will not forsake
the house of our God." This means two things that Nehemiah has discussed in this chapter. He places special emphasis
on faithfulness in giving. According to the law of Moses,
always they had to bring to the Lord the firstfruits of everything. In spite of very heavy taxation, Nehemiah reminded
them to see to it that the Lord received His firstfruits: to
use Jesus' own instruction in the New Testament, they were
to "Render . . . unto Caesar the things which are Caesar's;
and unto God the things that are God's" (Matthew 22:21).
I honestly believe that a great part of revival is faithfulness
in giving.

And then, in the second place, Nehemiah emphasizes
faithfulness in worship: ". . . we will not forsake the house
of our God." Probably that means not just that we will not
fail to attend it, but that we will not let it down. Faithfulness in giving will be accompanied by faithfulness in at-
tendance. Our worship can never enrich God, yet we rob
Him of His due if we fail to join with His people in worship.
If we do, we will suffer spiritual leanness, and if we suffer
spiritually that means there is a breakdown in our usefulness.

How can we have revival? We do not have to wait for
some miraculous intervention from heaven. Charles G.
Finney, of whom I am a great admirer, says that revival
comes by the right use of clearly defined means, and I am
sure he is right.

God's clearly defined means are just these things: our return to brokenheartedness (a tenderness of heart in which He can plant the seed of the Spirit); a reflection on God's goodness (a taking of time for meditation); a recognition of our sinfulness (an honest self-examination regarding sin); a renewal of our obedience (that puts revival into action).

May God bless that word to your heart and mine and lead us into that very experience.

12. Strategy and Surrender

And the rulers of the people dwelt at Jerusalem: the rest of the people also cast lots, to bring one of ten to dwell in Jerusalem the holy city, and nine parts to dwell in other cities.

And the people blessed all the men, that willingly offered themselves to dwell at Jerusalem. . . .

And the residue of Israel, of the priests, and the Levites, were in all the cities of Judah, every one in his inheritance.

But the Nethinims dwelt in Ophel: and Ziha and Gispa were over the Nethinims.

The overseer also of the Levites at Jerusalem was Uzzi the son of Bani, the son of Hashabiah, the son of Mattaniah, the son of Micha. Of the sons of Asaph, the singers were over the business of the house of God.

For it was the king's commandment concerning them, that a certain portion should be for the singers, due for every day. . . .

And at the dedication of the wall of Jerusalem they sought the Levites out of all their places, to bring them to Jerusalem, to keep the dedication with gladness, both with thanksgivings, and with singing, with cymbals, psalteries, and with harps.

And the sons of the singers gathered themselves together, both out of the plain country round about Jerusalem, and from the villages of Netophathi;

Also from the house of Gilgal, and out of the fields of Geba and Azmaveth: for the singers had builded them villages round about Jerusalem.

And the priests and the Levites purified themselves, and purified the people, and the gates, and the wall. . . .

Also that day they offered great sacrifices, and rejoiced: for God had made them rejoice with great joy: the wives also and the children rejoiced: so that the joy of Jerusalem was heard even afar off.

—Nehemiah 11:1, 2, 20-23; 12:27-30, 43.

THE FACT THAT not more than fifty thousand of God's people had returned from captivity in Persia and were dwelling in Jerusalem in Nehemiah's time left them particularly susceptible to attack. Numerically they were at a disadvantage, and would speedily need to learn the lesson that in spiritual warfare it is "Not by might, nor by power, but by my spirit, saith the Lord of hosts."

It would be the part of a wise executive to insure that each man was duly allotted to his appointed task, and that the best possible use was made of available personnel. To glance through the two chapters of Nehemiah under consideration is to recognize that there are three words which could be used to summarize the situation here and to reveal the strategy of this man's spiritual leadership.

The first word is "occupation." It was particularly important that the stronghold of Jerusalem should be manned by the best warriors, and therefore mighty men of valor were appointed to live in the city. It was planned that the princes should live there and that ten per cent of the people, selected by lot, should take up their residence there also.

There are principles here we all need to recognize and to apply to our own individual circumstances in Christian service. I believe the secret is in the words of Paul to the church at Ephesus, "But unto every one of us is given grace according to the measure of the gift of Christ" (Ephesians 4:7).

There are certain strategic areas that have to be held at all cost, and for these are needed men of proved valor. But they must be supported by others serving in their own appointed area and serving happily in the will of God. There is always grace given to us for any service which we undertake in His will, and I somehow think that the reason for so much unhappiness in Christian work is that many Christians spend much of their time envying the gifts of other people and the sphere of service allotted to them instead of happily serving the Lord in the task to which they themselves are called.

Every Christian is exposed to the attack of the enemy of souls in his service for the Lord—at least if he is serving in the will of God. I remember years ago I prayed, "Lord, never take me to any sphere of Christian work for Thee in which Satan is not interested, because if he isn't interested, then I surely could never be in Thy will." Believe me, that prayer has been answered a hundredfold, much more than I bargained for!

Nevertheless, in the will of God, Christian service is changed from drudgery to luxury by the experience of drawing upon His all-sufficient grace. I wonder if you experience that in your Christian work, or have you become easily discouraged, burdened about it in a worried and anxious kind of way, to the point that you feel that the only thing to do is to leave it all alone? Is it a tremendous strain and a great effort? Or are you finding in the midst of all the spiritual warfare that the Lord is adding more grace as the burdens grow greater, and to multiplied trials, His multiplied peace?

Yes, occupation in the sphere to which God has called

you, happily serving Him in His will, is a great secret of contentment in Christian work, and indeed also is the training which leads to enlarged capacity for His service.

The next word that seems to be suggested in these chapters is the word "delegation." Everyone had an appointed task, and everyone was cared for.

You will notice in Nehemiah 11:22, 23, that singers were over the business of the house of God, and it was the king's commandment concerning them that certain portions should be paid to them each day. These people might well have felt that they were quite useless, and that they were not contributing to the communal life at all, as they merely sang the praises of God. But as a matter of fact, they fulfilled a very important part in their ministry of encouraging the praise of God throughout the whole community.

I wonder if sometimes you feel that your life is quite obscure and useless. It does not seem that you have any particular gifts or any particular way in which you can serve the Lord. Maybe you have been laid aside for a long time, taken out of Christian work, and you feel yourself to be on the shelf, so to speak.

Some years ago, when I was preaching at a little church on the south side of London, I was asked to visit a young woman who had been completely paralyzed for nine years. Up to the age of twenty-one she had been an active worker in the church and Sunday school, and God seemed greatly to have blessed her ministry. But suddenly she was stricken with this dreadful disease and since that time had never been able to move.

I gladly assented to go to see her, but as I went along the road to the house I wondered to myself, "What can I say to this dear soul? I have never known anything about suffering like that." And it seems to me that before you can really bring comfort to others you have to know something of the experience through which they have passed.

So I asked that the Lord would give me some word to say to her that might be a blessing, and as I knocked on the door, her mother answered and led me into the sick room. There lay this young woman, absolutely helpless, on her back. I went up to her bedside and began to utter a word of sympathy. She looked at me, and I shall never forget the look in her face when she said, "Please don't offer your sympathy. I don't need it. I would not have missed the experience of these past nine years for anything in the world.

"When I was twenty-one years of age serving the Lord at church," she said, "I remember yielding my life completely to Him, saying to Him, 'Lord, I am ready for anything You may want me to do for You or be for You.' Only a few weeks later His hand touched my body and laid me aside. Through these past years He has become so infinitely more precious to me than He could ever have been in all the busy round of Christian service."

As I listened to her, I felt so utterly unworthy, and I wondered just how much I had suffered for Jesus. It seemed to me here was a young woman, quite out of the public eye, who had been not laid aside in sickness but called aside for stillness, so that during these nine years the Lord had drawn so very close to her, and she to Him.

I discovered that she had a long prayer list, and every day she spent hours in prayer for missionaries, preachers, and teachers of the Word. She put me on her prayer list that day, and eternity alone will reveal how much I owe as a minister of the gospel to the prayers of that dear woman who for so long had been helpless and crippled. Surely this is just one example out of thousands where the Lord has permitted the suffering and the crushing that out of such a life there might come fragrance and fruitfulness and inspiration to others.

I believe the King of kings has a very special portion for such dear souls because their ministry is so mighty and so effective. Delegation, yes, to a very precious task but a very costly one. I wonder if you and I would be willing to have it delegated to us? Just suppose every bit of Christian work we do were taken from us, that our health and strength departed, and we were laid aside like that. Would we be bitter, or could we accept such a thing as from the hand of the Lord?

Somehow I feel that some day when we see our Lord face to face there will be some great surprises. Many of us who have held prominent positions in Christian work may not be so prominent then. Many who have been obscure, lonely souls, to whom little attention has been paid and whose ministry has never been recognized or praised, will be among those who are the first to hear His "Well done!"

Let the principle be recognized that the most obscure task in the service of the King of kings is as important as the most public one when it is done in the will of God. Let there therefore be neither strife, nor envy, nor contempt, nor ill will between those who are the valiant men holding key positions and those who are doing the unseen, unrecognized, unreported tasks. Both are needful, both are useful, both are dependent upon each other, and neither can be spared.

Then the secret of victorious service in each of these fields depends upon the third word which is before us in these chapters, and that is the word "dedication."

Here was a very joyful occasion, so much so indeed that we are told that the joy of Jerusalem was heard even afar off (v. 43). Although the number of people who had returned to the land was small, nevertheless they had been brought to see that what really mattered in their lives was their relationship to the Lord.

Their joy that day in the dedication of the wall was the joy of the Lord. A great deal of material splendor that marked former years had gone, but surely now there could be a greater glory in their devotion to the will of God and surrender for His purpose. These things could make them far more powerful than ever they had been. The wall was built with a great deal of fear and trembling, but the dedication of it was the occasion for a great deal of joy and victory. Is not this what the psalmist said, "They that sow in tears shall reap in joy"?

Here, then, was a great day of thanksgiving to God for all His mercies in enabling them to complete the task; not only so, but it was a moment when they dedicated the city and themselves to God and to His glory. Whatever else might be done for their own personal comfort, first of all must be done that which would honor and glorify God. They sought to put the city and its walls under His protection, acknowledging that unless the Lord kept it, then their walls indeed were built in vain.

That sacred and blessed day of dedication touched every

heart. We are told in the thirtieth verse of the twelfth chapter that they purified themselves. This joy was more than skin deep, and there was nothing superficial about it. In any work of God that has to pass through our hands, may He grant that they may be clean and our hearts may be pure. Those of us who would be used in the hands of the Lord to bring blessing to others must sanctify ourselves and set ourselves apart for God with absolute sincerity and with intensity of purpose.

Not only did it touch their hearts, but that day also touched their pockets, and careful regulations were made for the due collection of tithes and offerings.

Yes, strategy in their warfare was matched by surrender in their lives, and both went to the uttermost limits. I wonder sometimes if this is not what is lacking in so many Christian circles today. Our strategy is not divinely planned and our surrender is incomplete. I want to remind you of these three words again: occupation, delegation, dedication—there is a tremendous connection between them.

To serve the Lord happily in His will, to recognize the equal importance of every task in His service—these things call for dedication that is complete, but they are not in themselves the factors which lead to dedicated living. Such commitment surely lies deeper. The dedication of these people was because of the mercies of God, and is it not true in each one of our lives that the motive for total surrender lies just there? As the Apostle Paul says, "I beseech you therefore, brethren, by the mercies of God, that ye present your bodies a living sacrifice, holy, acceptable unto God, which is your reasonable service" (Romans 12:1).

The mercies of God—yes, that is our motive. And as if

to use an example of the mercies of God, I find that in this
chapter the name of a man who owed everything to the
mercies of God is frequently repeated. No less than five
times is David brought to mind—how his influence has
remained with them through the years! In spite of all his
sin, he is yet described as a man of God, and of course that
is what he was.

Would you like to be known as a man of God? Then, like
David, give everything to God. The Lord said concerning
him, "I have found David the son of Jesse, a man after mine
own heart, who shall fulfil all my will" (Acts 13:22).

His consecration was complete—is yours? I'm afraid
that too many of us live a life of halfhearted consecration to
the Lord. A bit is given here and there, but never all of
ourselves. David surrendered himself to do all the will of
God, and he became a man after God's own heart.

As you look back on God's mercies in your life, would
you not make this a moment when, without reserve, and
holding nothing back, you yield entirely to Him for whatever His will may be?

Also, dedication is not simply yielding all—it is taking all.
Someone has said that it is not what we give to Jesus but
what we take from Him that makes us strong and victorious
day by day. To discover that in the Lord Jesus all the fullness of the Godhead dwells bodily, and to know that we
are complete in Him, to know that there is nothing we
need at all for life or character which is not in Him, and
held by Him for each one of us—that is His purpose for us.

The tragedy of our lives is that we take so little, and if
we are poor and miserable in Christian work and service,
we have nobody to blame but ourselves. It is a great thing

when in Christian work we realize that it is not only a question of yielding all to God, but of taking everything from Him.

Perhaps most of all we must recognize that we are called upon to be faithful stewards, using all we have for Him. That is the supreme and final aim in all dedication, that His glory might be revealed and that He might be magnified in us whether by life or by death.

Steward I—and not possessor—of the wealth entrusted me.
What, were God Himself the holder, would His disposition be?
This I ask myself each morning, every noon and every night
As I view His gentle goodness with an ever new delight.

Steward only—never owner of the time that He has lent.
How, were He my life custodian, would my years on earth be spent?
Thus I ask myself each hour, as I plod my pilgrim way
Steeped in gratefulest amazement at His mercy day by day.

Steward only—not possessor—of the part of Him that's I.
Clearer grows this truth and dearer as the years go slipping by.
May I softly go, and humbly, head and heart in reverence bent
That I may not fear to show Him how my stewardship was spent.

—Strickland Gillilan

You see, stewardship and dedication are not concerned simply with material things; they are concerned with the abandonment of ourselves utterly to the Lord. There is the key to spiritual strategy and the secret of surrender in all Christian service.

To be very practical, there are <u>four</u> different <u>spheres</u> which should feel the impact of such a dedication. The first is your <u>home,</u> which should be a sweeter and lovelier place just because you are living a dedicated life. It should be more than a restaurant or a domitory; rather, it should be a place where a spirit of dedication is worked out in loving Christian fellowship.

The second sphere is your <u>business.</u> If you are a dedicated Christian this ceases to be a job, for you are conscious that now you serve the Lord there. Believe me, it is no greater thing to serve the Lord on the mission field somewhere than to tap a typewriter if you are in God's will. No longer will you serve Him there with an eye on the clock; rather you will regard your business as much of a vocation as preaching the gospel, and your employer would be only too thankful if his whole staff were Christian.

The third sphere is your <u>country,</u> for a dedicated Christian will recognize that he has an obligation to the state. I believe there ought to be a new, flaming passion for social righteousness as there was in the days of the prophets. Too often, especially in fundamental circles, we are afraid of what we call the "social gospel," or the social implications of our gospel. The fact is that <u>the gospel of Jesus Christ should permeate every aspect of life.</u> The Christian church should be producing today Christian teachers, Christian statesmen, Christian lawyers; indeed, in every walk of life there ought to be men who know their God and who are strong to do exploits for Him.

The fourth sphere is your <u>church.</u> I believe most profoundly that any Christian who is not a member of a local church is out of the will of God. It is within the sphere of the local church that he can express to the best advantage the dedication and surrender of his life. The church urgently needs the prayer backing of every one of its members, the regular worship of the whole congregation, and the sacrificial giving of every child of God. I wonder if we have really carried this strategy and surrender far enough, if it has really permeated every part of our being. Are there still areas in your life in which Jesus Christ is not Lord and Sovereign, over which He has no control?

Oh, that in the recognition of all His mercies there may be the response of total dedication:

> Lord of every thought and action,
> Lord to send and Lord to stay,
> Lord in speaking, writing, giving,
> Lord in all things to obey.
> Lord of all there is of me
> Now and evermore to be.

13. A Grand Finale

On that day they read in the book of Moses in the audience of the people; and therein was found written, that the Ammonite and the Moabite should not come into the congregation of God for ever;

Because they met not the children of Israel with bread and with water, but hired Balaam against them, that he should curse them: howbeit our God turned the curse into a blessing.

Now it came to pass, when they had heard the law, that they separated from Israel all the mixed multitude.

And before this, Eliashib the priest, having the oversight of the chamber of the house of our God, was allied unto Tobiah:

And he had prepared for him a great chamber, where aforetime they laid the meat offerings, the frankincense, and the vessels, and the tithes of the corn, the new wine, and the oil, which was commanded to be given to the Levites, and the singers, and the porters; and the offerings of the priests.

But in all this time was not I at Jerusalem: for in the two and thirtieth year of Artaxerxes king of Babylon came I unto the king, and after certain days obtained I leave of the king:

And I came to Jerusalem, and understood of the evil that Eliashib did for Tobiah, in preparing him a chamber in the courts of the house of God.

And it grieved me sore: therefore I cast forth all the household stuff of Tobiah out of the chamber.

Then I commanded, and they cleansed the chambers: and thither brought I again the vessels of the house of God, with the meat offering and the frankincense.

—Nehemiah 13:1-9

In accordance with his agreement with the Persian king, Nehemiah had returned to the court upon the completion of the building of the wall. Twelve years later, seeking renewed permission, he returned to Jerusalem. The last chapter of this amazing record in the Word of God reveals to us the unswerving loyalty of Nehemiah to his God, right through to the very end.

"And I came to Jerusalem, and understood . . ." (v. 7).

Those few words are the clue to the whole zeal and character of this man Nehemiah. He came to Jerusalem, the place from which all divine strategy in the world was yet to be conducted, the center of God's operations, the Holy City, and there he understood—he saw clearly God's purpose for His people. He saw that God's intention was to reach the multitude through the few, that <u>God is</u> not <u>concerned</u> with crowds, but <u>with channels,</u> and that the <u>channels must be clean and pure.</u>

Nehemiah was the last historian of Old Testament times; only four hundred years more and then the Messiah would come. He knew that God wanted His people to fulfill His purpose in the world. He understood also their failure, and this chapter tells us the tragic story of what had happened.

You recall that the people had met in a great convention to worship God. They had made a covenant with the Lord, and the stage seemed set for abiding blessing. But no, the

same sins which had ruined their national life before their
captivity had attacked again and overcome them.

What were they? They were three in number. In the first
place, there was the mingling with other nations—failure
in separation. In the second place there was a desecration
of the Sabbath day—failure in service. And in the third
place there were marriages with heathen people—failure in
sanctification.

On Nehemiah's return to Jerusalem, he found all of
these things being practiced. Tobiah the Ammonite, their
bitter enemy who had opposed constantly the building of
the wall, was comfortably housed in the court of God's
house, the very man whom Nehemiah had told that he had
no part nor lot in Jerusalem. Furthermore, all sorts of business and traffic were going on on the Lord's day. Worse
still, one of the sons of the priests had married the daughter
of Sanballat. There were three cheers in hell—once again
the enemy was strongly entrenched in Jerusalem!

But with Nehemiah back on the scene, things began to
move! All Tobiah's furniture was thrown out on the street,
and himself with it.

The gates of the city were shut on the evening before the
Sabbath day. Some who dared sell their goods outside the
wall were warned off with the threat of a sound thrashing
from Nehemiah. The record tells us that "From that time
forth, came they no more on the sabbath." I should think
they didn't!

Those who were guilty of unholy alliances with "outlandish" women suffered at the hands of Nehemiah. He
". . . contended with them, and cursed them, and smote

certain of them, and plucked off their hair. . . ." What a man!

Perhaps you think he was too severe. Not at all! He understood, for now he knew that God's purposes depended upon a holy people. God must have them at any cost; He must have the few who were truly clean and right with Him that the world might be reached. God is still the same today, and through the few He plans to reach the world. Do you not long to be among that number?

Let me put the words of this text on the lips of One of whom Nehemiah is only a picture. *He* came to Jerusalem and He understood. Yes, two thousand years ago Jesus Christ came: He understood the purpose of His Father— and He also understood the failure and sinfulness of man.

The Old Testament was full of promises made by men, promises which were broken. Jesus Christ came that the New Testament might be full of promises made by God which would be kept. He came that the Holy Spirit might dwell in us to give us victory, and to make us pure channels through whom He can reach the lost. He went away for a while, and today He comes to make your heart and mine the center of His operations, the place of all His activities, for He alone understands the purpose of God for us.

But what does He see?

Does He see failure in separation? What Tobiah has wormed his way into the center of your life and sits there comfortably enthroned where the Lord Jesus ought to be? What furniture is cluttering up the temple which the Holy Spirit ought to fill, and causing loud cheers in hell? Is it not a fact that in so many instances Christian people have so little room for the Holy Spirit because they have allowed so many other things to crowd into their lives?

In the north of Ireland there is a little town called Ballymena. It is a very Protestant town, and the Christian people there are very fond of holding cottage meetings. On one occasion a lady planned a series of three cottage meetings to be held in her home weekly.

Her next-door neighbor happened to be one of the few Roman Catholics who lived in that town, and she duly received an invitation to attend the meeting. She made an excuse and said she could not come, but the following morning she was interested enough to inquire if the meeting had gone well.

"Oh yes," the hostess said. "We had a wonderful time. We had thirty-five people in my little home, and it was full. Won't you come next week?"

"No," was the reply. "I'm sorry, but I really cannot."

The next week the meeting was held again and the following morning a similar conversation took place.

"Did you have a good time last night?"

"Yes, a very good time, even better than last week. We had fifty-one people and my little cottage was full. There will be one more meeting next week. Will you come?"

"No, I really must not. I'm sorry."

The third meeting came and went, and the following day the same question was asked across the garden wall.

"Did you have a good meeting last night?" asked the Roman Catholic lady.

"Oh yes, wonderful!" said her neighbor. "The very best yet. We had sixty-two people in my little cottage, and it was absolutely full."

Well, that was just too much for the Roman Catholic, who protested, "But that's a sheer impossibility. You began your meetings with thirty-five people, and you said then that your house was full. The next week it was fifty-one, and last night sixty-two. That just can't be done! It doesn't make sense!"

"Oh yes, it does," said her friend. "It is very simple. Of course our little house was full when we had thirty-five in it, but you see, last night we just put all the furniture out on the lawn and made room for sixty-two."

What a parable that is! How much room is there in your life for the Holy Spirit? Is the whole trouble that Tobiah and his furniture clutter up the place? Then they need to be thrown out, promptly and firmly.

What about your bookshelves? Would the divine approval be upon all that is there? What about your clothes closet? Did you pray before you purchased all its contents? Would it be something upon which the Lord would smile? Is it designed to attract to yourself or attract to Jesus? What about your record collection? Would He be satisfied with all that is there? Or would He have to put His finger upon something that should be thrown out?

My dear fellow Christians, if you mean business for God in these desperate days, I suggest to you we need an examination of every part of our lives so that the furniture with which the enemy clutters them up might be thrown out. Oh, that we would learn to make room for God to work!

But again, has there been a failure in service? What traffic goes on in your heart which destroys that Sabbath of rest and peace? What thoughts invade that temple of your body? And what about your service for the Lord upon

His day? Is not that one of the great tragedies even in con-
servative Christian circles in this country? We attend Sunday school and church, but we give the rest of the day to
television, to boating on the lake, to picnics, to excursions,
to anything under the sun except faithfulness to the house
of God. Some just never think of their responsibility to
invite a friend who does not know the Lord to the house
of God for the evening service. Is there breakdown there
in your life?

What about failure in sanctification? Tell me, is there
some unholy alliance in your life which threatens to destroy your testimony? Do you cherish some friendship that
is clearly outside the will of God because it is contrary
to the Word of God? What daughter of Sanballat has
captured your affection and stolen the loyalty of your heart
from the Saviour Himself? I wonder what "outlandish" man
or woman has taken you from Him? What Delilah has taken
away your spiritual strength?

How many, many times a young man or woman has
entered into marriage out of God's will with a partner who
is not a Christian, and has said, "I'll win her (or him) for
Christ when we are married." But it never works that way,
and almost without exception the result is disaster.

If you would live godly in this world you will have to
break the heart of someone, believe me. Very frequently,
in order to obey the will of the Lord, the heart you break
is that of someone dear to you, perhaps the heart of your
father or mother, some member of your family, your sweetheart. That is what Jesus said would happen: "Suppose ye
that I am come to give peace on earth? I tell you, Nay; but
rather division: For from henceforth there shall be five

in one house divided, three against two, and two against three. The father shall be divided against the son, and the son against the father; the mother against the daughter, and the daughter against the mother; the mother in law against her daughter in law, and the daughter in law against her mother in law" (Luke 12:51-53).

Better break anybody's heart than break the heart of God! In any event, how blessedly true it is that to obey the will of God results ultimately in blessing in the lives of those who at the moment of decision we seem to hurt. To refuse to accept the path of God's call, to lower the standard in Christian life in order to make things more easy in terms of human affection is always disaster, not only to ourselves, but also to those concerned. But to go through with the will of God and to do that which seems to be ruthless and even unkind in order to obey God at any cost is ultimately the way to win others for the Lord.

These are no times for half-measures. Has there been failure in your separation, failure in your service, failure in your sanctification? Is there great glee in the regions beneath, because the channel which God intended to use in your life is choked? Yes, the Lord Jesus comes to the Jerusalem of your heart and He understands. Would you let Him throw out the idol, silence the traffic which disturbs the peace and rest of your heart? Would you be willing for Him to break off the unholy alliance?

Remember the God of Nehemiah is our God. Disobedience to Him always brings punishment. Sin brings slavery, but repentance always brings the outpouring of His mercy and blessing. And the Holy Spirit filling the life that has been emptied of furniture always brings victory, for He

is the Victor. To be quick in understanding the fear of God
and the will of God is always to be merciless to everything
that is contrary to the will of God, no matter how much
it hurts.

Do you notice in this chapter that three times Nehemiah
prayed that the Lord would remember him? I do not
think for a moment that he expected to buy God's favor
because of his faithfulness to the Lord. But rather, being
himself one who trusted the Lord, Nehemiah humbly asked
that the work that he did might come under remembrance
before God.

I think this is a very wonderful thing, that every one of us
may remember the word of our Lord Jesus, ". . . thou hast
been faithful over a few things, I will make thee ruler over
many things. . . ." To serve Him here for a reward is not our
motive, but it is a tremendous strength in the battle to know
that one day there is a "Well done" awaiting us if we have
been faithful to Him.

As I look back upon this classic book on Christian service,
the Book of Nehemiah, I see a man who was faithful to the
very end. And, of course, that is what counts: not how I
begin, but how I end.

I am reminded of the verse in the sixth chapter of Ephesians as translated by Weymouth (v. 13), "Therefore put on
the complete armor of God, so that you may be able to
stand your ground in the evil day, and having fought to the
end, to remain victors on the field."

Yes, that is what counts. We are all engaged in an intense
spiritual warfare in which there will be no armistice until
we reach heaven. Satan hurls all his fiery darts at the child
of God who is abandoned to the will of God, and at the

church which is concerned to have a soul-winning ministry. This will mean that in the course of the battle there will be grave wounds, much suffering and hurt, many things that grieve us and break our hearts, but nothing matters except that we should stand our ground and remain victorious on the field.

What a day it will be when the Lord welcomes us home! Indeed, it will be worth it all when we see Jesus. We will understand then, as we can never understand now, that the very wounds which so often have been inflicted upon us have been the means of conforming us to the image of the Lord Jesus, and of making Him all the more precious to us.

Circumstances which we have resented, situations which we have found desperately difficult, have all been the means in the hands of God of driving the nails into the self-life which so easily complains. His dealing causes us to rejoice in the midst of affliction, "For our light affliction, which is but for a moment, worketh for us a far more exceeding and eternal weight of glory" (II Corinthians 4:17).

Just as one day Nehemiah came to Jerusalem and understood, and just as the Lord Jesus comes to the Jerusalem of our hearts and understands, so, praise God, we shall come to the heavenly Jerusalem and understand, for ". . . then shall I know even as also I am known" (I Corinthians 13:12).

O Jesus, I have promised to serve Thee to the end;
Be Thou forever near me, my Master and my Friend;
I shall not fear the battle if Thou art by my side,
Nor wander from the pathway if Thou wilt be my guide.

O let me feel Thee near me! the world is ever near;
I see the sights that dazzle, the tempting sounds I hear:

My foes are ever near me, around me and within;
But, Jesus, draw Thou nearer, and shield my soul from sin.

O Jesus, Thou hast promised to all who follow Thee,
That where Thou art in glory there shall Thy servant be;
And, Jesus, I have promised to serve Thee to the end;
O give me grace to follow, my Master and my Friend.

—John E. Bode

FIRST UNITED PRESBYTERIAN CHURCH
2619 BROADWAY
OAKLAND 12, CALIFORNIA